Pathway_{to} Purpose™

for women

PATHWAY TO PURPOSE™ SERIES

Pathway to Purpose™ for Women

Conversations on Purpose for Women

Praying for Purpose for Women

Pathway to Purpose™ for Women Abridged Audio CD

Pathway to Purpose™ for Women Personal Journal

Pathway *to* Purpose

for women

connecting your to-do list,
your passions, and God's
purposes for your life

KATIE BRAZELTON

ZONDERVAN™

GRAND RAPIDS, MICHIGAN 49530 USA

ZONDERVAN™

Pathway to Purpose™ for Women

Copyright © 2005 by Katherine F. Brazelton

This title is also available as a Zondervan audio product. Visit www.zondervan.com/audiopages for more information.

Requests for information should be addressed to:

Zondervan, *Grand Rapids, Michigan 49530*

ISBN-10: 0-310-26587-8

ISBN-13: 978-0-310-6587-0

International Trade Paper Edition

Interior design by Beth Shagene

Printed in the United States of America

05 06 07 08 09 10 11 12 /❖ DCI/ 10 9 8 7 6 5 4 3 2 1

To my precious daughter, Stephanie,
who encouraged me for fifteen years,
"Mom, God wants you to do this."
For endless months, you did my chores,
ran my errands, bought our groceries,
and even did a hospital visit for me!

To my remarkable son, Andy,
who constantly said in words
and countless kind gestures,
"Don't you dare give up.
What you're doing for women matters."

To Julie, Andy's amazing wife,
who has been a jewel to me
during this writing process.

You three precious souls kept me amply supplied
with prayers, love, hugs, notes, and hope.
Because of you three, I lacked no good thing.
I thank you for being Jesus to me as I answered
God's call on my life.

I love you to pieces. May your witness
of the unfolding of God's purposes in my life
vividly remind you that he has an unparalleled plan
for you as well. My prayer is to be used by God
day-by-day as "wind beneath your wings."

May you each soar on wings like eagles.

Isaiah 40:31

You've got my feet on the life-path,
with your face shining sun-joy all around.
(ACTS 2:28, MSG)

Contents

Part Five

RUN TO JESUS

God's *Worship* Purpose for You: To Magnify Him with Your Life

Part Six

POINT OTHERS TOWARD THE PATHWAY

God's *Evangelism* Purpose for You: To Complete His Mission for Your Life

APPENDIXES

How to Use the Pathway to Purpose™ Series

In 2002, my dear pastor, Rick Warren, wrote *The Purpose-Driven® Life*, which sends up a clarion call for people to live out God's five purposes:

- FELLOWSHIP (connecting with others)
- DISCIPLESHIP (knowing Christ and becoming like him)
- MINISTRY (serving others)
- WORSHIP (magnifying God with your life)
- EVANGELISM (completing God's mission for your life in the world)

If you haven't already read this phenomenal bestseller, I highly recommend it. I also recommend that your church go through the powerful 40 Days of Purpose campaign.

All the books in the Pathway to Purpose™ series work together to help you daily embrace the five universal purposes as you discover your individual God-given calling.

Pathway to Purpose™ for Women, the main book in the series, shows you how to connect your to-do list, your passions, and God's purposes for your life. How do you live through—see through—the *ordinary* when you yearn for your own *significant* purpose? Discover how God has uniquely designed you and used your life experiences to prepare you for your specific calling. If you can only read one of the three books, this is the one to read. (This book also is available as an Abridged Audio CD.)

- *Personal use*—Each chapter ends with a Bible exploration and personal questions.
- *Small Group and Retreat use*—See the Group Discussion Guide in the back of the book.

Conversations on Purpose for Women is designed for the reader of *Pathway to Purpose for Women* who wants to go deeper. This workbook encourages you to choose a Purpose Partner and make ten appointments with each other. Enjoy conversation starters, Scripture verses, questions, and specific self-assessment exercises that help you unpack God's unique purpose for your life, from an initial sneak preview to the most challenging steps of your journey.

- *Personal use with your Purpose Partner*—Find a partner and enjoy fellowship and growth while exploring God's specific life purposes together.
- *Small Group and Retreat use*—Work through the book as a small group, women's Sunday school class, or in a retreat setting by dividing into groups of three to four maximum and completing and discussing the exercises at paced intervals.

Praying for Purpose for Women is a sixty-day prayer experience that guides you as you ask God to reveal your life's purposes. You will discover insights from modern-day role models and biblical characters, specific questions to ask yourself as you seek God's answers, and an eye-opening analysis of your life patterns and purposes.

- *Personal use*—This book can be used by itself as a daily devotional. However, if you use it as a devotional while reading *Pathway to Purpose for Women*, your whole experience will be deepened and solidified.

• *Retreat use*—Ideal for a solitude retreat. Women can work through the book at their own pace during the weekend. On the last day together, they can pair up to discuss their findings, regardless of how far they got in the book.

Also available:

Pathway to Purpose™ for Women Personal Journal

As you search for and discover God's unique purpose for your life, it is important to record "what the Lord has done" in your family life, your personal life, and your ministry life. Each page in this companion book to *Pathway to Purpose for Women* will guide your journaling and allow you to reflect on how God is directing you on the pathway of your life.

SERIES FOREWORD

In 1997 Katie facilitated a two-day LifePlan for me and I found the experience highly significant—a turning point!

Up until then, I had been frustrated and confused about my spiritual gifts and goals, and unclear about the contribution my life would make for God's kingdom. Through Katie's firm-yet-gentle guidance, I viewed my life with new eyes and discovered a greater appreciation for God. Using large sheets of butcher paper hanging in her living room, we traced the path I had taken from childhood, and it became crystal-clear that God had been directing me at every point. I was humbled and convinced of his love for me. Things I knew intellectually moved from my head to my heart, and I was able to find joy and meaning in pain I had experienced.

The Holy Spirit used Katie to open my eyes to attitudes, sins, and wrong desires that I had been holding on to, and through a healing prayer time, I was able to release them. After reviewing the past and confirming the present, she drew from me the blue-sky dreams I had for my future . . . dreams I had been afraid to say out loud. In Katie's warm, gracious, encouraging presence, I invited God to use me in ways I never expected, never thought possible, and never even dared to hope. Our tears mingled as she affirmed God's call on my life, her belief that God had allowed the pain for his good purposes, and her faith in my ability to actually fulfill the God-inspired goals and dreams articulated in our time together.

Years later, many of those lessons still affect my daily life. God has taken me up on my offer to be used by him, and though the task often seems more than I can handle, I think back to those hours of breakthrough and am reassured that HE is directing my steps and HE will finish the work.

Katie brings this same warmth, gentle firmness, deep conviction, and passion for God to her books. You may never have the privilege of calling her "friend" as I do, but through her writings, you will find a dear companion for your spiritual journey.

Kay Warren
Saddleback Church
November 2004

Part One

Step
toward the
Pathway

Chapter 1

Is Your Life Out of Sync?

My life flies by—day after hopeless day.
(Job 7:6, TLB)

Do you remember George Bailey, the main character in the classic movie, *It's a Wonderful Life*? He sinks into a serious depression and even considers ending his life because of his unrealized dreams and feelings of uselessness. With the help of Clarence, an angel, George is shown the impact of the specific relational assignments in which he has been critically needed over the years. He comes to realize that there has been a clear purpose in his life all along. He discovers that his life has mattered and still matters a great deal.

Like George, we each have purposes to fulfill, many of which are linked to our relationships, passions, talents, experiences, dreams, hopes, and longings. Living a larger, more fulfilling and dynamic life than you may currently be living is possible when you catch God's vision for your life. It is a transformational experience. I'm no angel, but I experienced a remarkable transformation as I journeyed on the pathway to purpose. And, I am eager to share lessons I have learned along the way.

At age thirty-five, I unexpectedly found myself divorced. Gary and I had started dating during college. We got married, built a life together, had children. Then, in the flash of a conversation that lasted only a few minutes, it was over. All of a sudden I had no husband to tend to, my two children were often visiting their dad, and many of the family responsibilities that for years had defined my life were nearly nonexistent.

I was far more fortunate than many divorced women with young children. I was not financially abandoned and forced into survival mode. Quite the opposite. My ex-husband adored our children. He couldn't get enough of them or do enough to make our lives easier. So when the kids came home to me, they were fed, often newly clothed, and happily exhausted. I had less laundry, cooking, shopping, and homework assistance to worry about than when we were together as a family. I lived like a *divorced princess.*

But deep inside, I was not well. The ease of my life did nothing to lessen the immeasurable sadness of the divorce. My heart was broken and I was lonely. Fewer neighborhood kids visited our new, tiny house, and no couples invited me to join their outings. After a few bad experiences, I chose not to date. So I lived a quiet and simple life shared with several faithful friends, my Bible, and my new best companion, *TV Guide.*

With no pressing roles to fulfill, I felt enormously dispirited and useless. Everything I had crowded into my life to bring it some semblance of meaning had been yanked away or grown stagnant. My casual friends noticed that I seemed lost, but those who knew me best realized that I was crashing into hopelessness.

The pain of that transition and my lack of purpose was made worse by the fact that for five years I had begged God to give me a Joan of Arc–type cause or a unique purpose to champion, but he had not seen fit to do so. I felt confused. At times I wondered if the only logical life purpose I had left was shopping for new clothes because my weight spiraled downward as my depression deepened.

A Longing for Purpose

It has been more than a decade and a half since those difficult days, and God has given me more meaning in life than I ever could have imagined. In the midst of that purposeless desert, I began an intense spiritual journey through which God slowly revealed to me his multi-faceted reasons for my existence. Today, my service as a licensed minister at Saddleback Church and as a Certified Christian LifePlan Facilitator[1] allow me the privilege of walking alongside other women who are crying out for purpose in their lives.

I will share a bit more of my journey on the pathway to purpose shortly, but now, let me ask about you. How are you doing in the area of personal validity and life significance? Are you crying out to the Lord for clarity regarding his purposes for your life?

> *The whole life of the good Christian is a holy longing.*
> SAINT AUGUSTINE

Through my own faltering steps and my interaction with thousands of other women, I have come to realize that countless good, Christian women barely function because they feel alone, disillusioned, or trapped by vague dissatisfaction. They feel that they have no critically important reason to exist, and they are guilt-ridden about their dark secret of borderline despair.

The fact is, most women have felt this void at one time or another, even if just mildly. At some transition point in life, they have experienced a let-down feeling. This unexplainable melancholy may manifest itself in many ways—from the baby blues to a midlife crisis. It may be prompted by a job loss, a home relocation, or divorce. It may also occur after reaching a cherished goal such as completing a race, building a house, graduating from school, planning a wedding, or retiring from a career.

If you find yourself in this perplexing place, you may feel bored and confused. Perhaps you hunger for something challenging to which to give your life. Perhaps you began adulthood with great ideas of how you were going to make a difference in the world but now find yourself struggling to make sense of feelings of emptiness, frustration, or futility. Perhaps you can't turn off the unsettling questions that scream out in the silence of your nights:

- Dear God, where do I fit? How can I make a difference? Where is the place you have for me?

- Does anyone really need me? Does my existence even matter in this world?

- Why do I feel like such a failure as a Christian?

- Why don't I enjoy my church ministry, my family responsibilities, or my job anymore? Why do I feel so unsatisfied?

- Why am I not happy? How did I pile up so many regrets?

- Is this really all there is to life? Is this what God wants my life to look like?

- When did my dreams and passions get relegated to a back burner?

- If I heard God's call, would I have the time or emotional strength to pursue it?

If you find yourself facing questions like these and long for something better, be assured that there is hope. God will reveal your purpose, and your heart will sing over what he has in store for you! He wants you to be able to say, "I'm in my element. I'm in sync. This is what my life is supposed to be about. I was born for this. What a blast!" Or—the clincher in the case of a career—"I can't believe I get paid to do this!"

DESPERATE FOR ANSWERS

Let me share a little more of how I began my search for meaning in life. During those terrible days of feeling utterly purposeless, my life-long friend Beth and I talked about our similar frustrations. Both of us felt that, even though we had given our lives to Christ, he hadn't shown up lately (at least from our limited perspective!) to give us an updated and clear life direction. We longed for God to show us the way we should go, which we knew he could do.[2] We even joked about inventing a "purpose Geiger counter," so we could detect even the slightest signs of purposeful activity.

Beth had recently turned the Big Five-O and was an empty-nester. She described herself as a "worn-out married woman who was lost in a marsh of mediocrity, sinking in the quicksand of the quitter years." I felt more on edge, as if I was waiting for someone (or something) important who was never going to show up—much like waiting for a plumber on New Year's Eve.

Everyone handles this type of psychological and spiritual angst differently, depending on how mild or intense its manifestation. I was desperate. I didn't know how to ask for directions for my trek through the uncharted waters of purposelessness. I knew only that I was in bad mental and spiritual shape. I needed to do something—anything—to get unstuck. I knew I needed to take a bold step—any bold step—and see what awaited me.

I never expected my journey to begin as it did. My mom gave me a video of the life of Mother Teresa.[3] I watched it a half dozen times, crying each time as it touched me to the depth of my soul. On the video, Mother Teresa said that if God was calling me to serve him in a specific way, I would know it beyond a shadow of a doubt. She then extended an invitation to come to Calcutta.

I took her seriously and wrote a brief letter to the Missionaries of Charity in India asking for permission to visit. I knew those angels of mercy obediently answered God's call on their lives by ministering to the poorest of the poor in one of the most chaotic environments in the world. I figured that by working alongside women so in

> *In all of our hearts lies a longing for a Sacred Romance . . . this heart yearning set within us, the longing for transcendence; the desire to be part of something larger than ourselves. . . . The deepest part of our heart longs to be bound together in some heroic purpose with others of like mind and spirit.*[4]
> BRENT CURTIS AND JOHN ELDREDGE

tune with God I would find their secret to heeding his voice. Surely hearing their fascinating stories about how he had worked faithfully in their lives would help me gain insight about his plan for my own life.

They agreed that I could visit, and I began planning my trip to Calcutta. One decision involved my sixty-seven-year-old mom, who insisted on going with me. I had no idea how I could protect her from malaria, muggers, and mayhem, but she would not be dissuaded. Her mission to seek out and meet Mother Teresa was set in stone. As she phrased it, "I'm going, even if my chances of meeting that saintly woman are slim." I finally stopped trying to explain that the odds were stacked against our even seeing her beloved heroine. I laughed to myself as I recalled an old saying: "If it's not one thing, it's a mother!"

> *Can we let go of our well-worn paths and follow the one less traveled? . . . Discovering destiny is far from passive.*[5]
> BILL THRALL, BRUCE McNICOL, AND KEN McELRATH

So, my ex-husband whisked off our children on a much-anticipated vacation, and my mom and I donned backpacks and headed out on a ten-day trip that would have ripple effects through our lives. I boarded the plane with a mingled sense of apprehension and excitement. I wondered whether or not I would like the answers I found across the ocean. In any case, I was thankful to have a faithful and easygoing traveling companion like my mom. In a way she was my personal angel of mercy, a true treasure from God, who supported me in my efforts to understand my new life.

FIRST STEP, INDIA

Emerging from the airport after a fatiguing series of flights, I hailed an airport taxi. My heart pounded as our driver dodged rickshaws, trolleys, buses, taxicabs, cows, and pedestrians. I knew Calcutta had a population of eleven million, including more than sixty thousand homeless people, but that knowledge did not prepare me for the squalor of the streets. I saw dilapidated shacks made of bamboo, paper, plastic, mud, cardboard, and tires. I scanned the faces of women making cow dung patties to use as cooking fuel. I saw children relieving themselves in the gutters and recoiled at the sight of others using the same gutter water for bathing. My mom and I could only stare at each other in shock when we were dropped off in an alleyway near the Missionaries of Charity Mother House.

As the convent door opened, we were dumbstruck by an entirely different sight. A dozen noisy novices dressed in blue-and-white saris greeted us and cheerfully ushered us inside. Even as we were still sorting out our emotions, one of the sisters nonchalantly asked us, "Would you like to meet *Mother*?" We were speechless. The sister escorted us upstairs.

The experience was beyond surreal. Barefoot Mother Teresa bowed as we approached. She was small in stature and her shoulders were hunched over, yet she stood before us like a giant. When I saw her, Isaiah 61:3 flooded into my mind: "They will be called oaks of righteousness, a planting of the LORD for the display of his splendor."

My mom and I were well aware of this giant oak's reputation as a visionary servant-leader and of her work with lepers and the destitute. So we were surprised when she asked us to sit with her on a rickety wooden bench on an upstairs balcony. As we huddled together, she thanked us for coming to serve and for bringing supplies for the orphans. We chatted casually until I blurted out the question that was burning in my heart: "How can you do this work in these terrible slum conditions?"

A smile spread slowly across her face and into her eyes. She exuded Christlike gentleness as she touched my arm and whispered, "It's pure joy."[6]

I didn't know what to think. How could she say it is pure joy to work in the slums? Surely, this was meant to be a riddle of some kind—or was it the profound answer of a mature oak with deep roots? I wondered whether I would ever be able to figure out what she meant. Could her remark possibly hold a clue to the calm and direction for which I searched?

The trip to India was a dream-come-true for my mom. For that, I was thrilled. As for me, I wrongly concluded that Mother Teresa's pure joy came from the fact that she had a bold and intense purpose in life that made her *feel good* about her immense contribution. During the next decade that theory would prove to be false. I had so much to think about, but at least I had taken the first step on my search for purpose.

SECOND STEP, FRANKL

A year after my visit to Calcutta, I was sitting in graduate school (doodling) when the professor began to lecture about Dr. Viktor Frankl, a Nazi concentration camp survivor. He said that Frankl gave verbal injections of purpose to fellow prisoners on the verge of dying from hopelessness. Sometimes Frankl helped them hang on for the purpose of finishing a painting when they got home or planting a garden or hugging a loved one.

My internal purpose-finder went off at full volume, and I sat up in my chair as if electricity were running through my back. I listened intently as my professor explained the vital role of purpose in the human heart. And, even though he never mentioned our Creator God as the one who assigns purpose to each of us, I knew that my search for purpose was a God-designed phenomenon of human nature. My longing for significance finally made sense to me. I wasn't crazy, after all!

God *intends* for people to be driven by purpose! He *expects* us to seek definition to our existence and to listen closely while he reveals it. In his wisdom, he gave each of us varying degrees of the need to feel visible, to feel that we matter, to feel that we are making a contribution. No matter where we appear to be in life, whether we wear our emotions of purposelessness on our sleeve or the world thinks we have it all together, our longing for purpose still exists to some degree.

I zoned into my research mode to delve deeper. I didn't know where God was taking me, but the more I learned, the more passionate I became about Christians today understanding their purposes. I began to write volumes of disjointed insights. I had embarked again on the journey of my heart to find purpose in life.

THIRD STEP, SADDLEBACK

Several years after that classroom revelation, God orchestrated that my kids and I would begin attending Saddleback Church. I knew I had come home when Pastor Rick Warren began talking about God's purposes for the church and our lives. As he got to know me better, he once said that I, like many others, needed a regular *purpose transfusion* to keep functioning!

And today, thanks to God speaking through his Word and my pastor, I can get my daily supply of purpose. I learned that my God-given purposes are the same as yours. God designed each one of us to connect with others, know and become more like Christ, serve in ministry, magnify him with our lives, and share the good news of the gospel. My clearer understanding of those purposes has recalibrated every aspect of my life, including why it is such an honor to invest in my daily roles, why it is so important for me to mature spiritually, and what God is revealing to me about my unique purpose on earth.

After considering everything I had learned from my Calcutta days forward, I decided that life purpose has a *Do-Be-Do* ring to it: *Do* today what God is asking me to do today in my family, church, and community. *Be* more like Christ. And then, *do* the distinct and bold work God has specifically designed for me to do before I die! With that truth as the foundation, my challenge—and yours—is to discover the exciting specifics of this Do-Be-Do reality in our own lives.

LIFE STEPS TOWARD PURPOSE

Finding our life purpose is rarely easy. For most of us, myself included, it is the result of much perseverance and, at times, exhausting effort. In addition, it is not something most of us do well on our own, and I certainly could not have done it without the help of my younger sister, Maureen. She taught me the value of following a proven pathway, complete with mile markers, no matter what the goal.

What I learned from Maureen at first had nothing to do with my search for purpose in life. It had to do with my physical condition, specifically the lingering flabbiness still haunting me from my pregnancies. Maureen had completed twenty-seven marathons and three triathlons, including an Ironman competition in Hawaii. So I asked her to be my exercise coach and help me to get back in shape.

During our first training session, she simply instructed me to walk past one house and jog past the next. I began to do so on a regular basis, huffing and complaining, until I could run three entire blocks at a fairly nice clip.

Then Maureen said, "If you can run three blocks, you should try a 5K [3.1 miles] fun race." So I trained hard and crossed the finish line just to show her that I too could earn a T-shirt.

Then she challenged me, "If you can run a 5K, you can run a 10K [6.2 miles]." So I logged many more miles with her on practice runs and in races because I enjoyed her company.

I'm sure you can predict what she said next: "If you can run 10Ks, you can run a half-marathon [13.1 miles]." So, I plodded along and did just that because I noticed the added benefit of losing weight. (The ladies' chorus sang, "Amen!")

I eventually ran a half-marathon up hilly terrain in extreme summer heat and won a second-place medal. When the race director announced my name and put the medal around my neck, do you think it mattered to me that only one other woman in my age division had entered the race? No, I had won a medal!

I actually ran an extra mile after that race, trying to catch my sister when she goaded me, "If you can run a half-marathon uphill in the heat, you can run a marathon [26.2 miles]." Believe me, if I had been fast enough to tackle her, I would have made her take it back. I had had enough. But she had a power I did not. Armed with perspective and a strategic plan, she had been unrelenting about moving me to each new level of competition. Although I soon forgave her, I couldn't forget her most recent challenge.

So, in partnership with her, it was not long before I ran my first marathon. I was tough to the core through mile eighteen. Then I hit the infamous *wall*:

Mile 18—sucked down Gatorade to keep up my energy

Mile 19—asked people to throw cups of water on me

Mile 20—doubled over in hunger pangs and cried like a baby

Mile 21—said, "Talk to me . . . no, don't talk to me"

Mile 22—made deals with God to make it end

Mile 23—asked my sister to push me along from behind

Mile 24—was too tired to complain

Mile 25—screamed in anger and pain that the race was sheer madness

Mile 26—inched along, begging, "Somebody shoot me"

Mile 26.2—sprinted to the finish line at 3 hours and 59 minutes

Mile 26.3—collapsed on the grass after the race and laughed aloud with joy!

Despite my *wall* experience, that marathon and several that followed were highlights of my life. I credit much of the success to my sister, my coach, who clearly understood the process of training for the long haul. Her knowledge regarding each step of the process and her ability to inspire me made it possible for her to pull (and push) me toward the goal.

I find a great similarity between a novice trying to run a marathon and a woman trying to find her life purposes. In both scenarios, you need a guide or partner who understands the entire pathway of where you want to go, one who can prepare you for the challenges and risks that lie ahead. Many women fail to discover and fulfill their significant life purposes because they have no Christian mentor, trainer, adviser, or tutor who can instruct them in the proper steps to reach the next mile marker.

If you have a strong desire to eliminate emptiness, fear, boredom, and meaninglessness from your life, let me be your *Maureen*. Journey with me to discover how each step toward living out God's purposes for your life will both challenge and exhilarate you. Come with me to where you can get a clear view of the life your heavenly Father has always intended you to live, where your life has significant meaning, your relationships are authentic, and your inner peace is deep.

It won't be an easy path to maneuver, but let's hike it together. Let's count on God to provide the stepping-stones that lead to the discovery of his daily purposes and unique, long-term purpose for your life. When you feel that God is nudging you to move forward, please join me on this incomparable adventure along God's pathway to purpose.

Notes

1. (p. 19) A LifePlan consultation is a private, two-day, Holy Spirit driven, same-sex facilitation during which a client asks God, "What is your will for the next season of my life and the second half of my life?" (See Chapter 13, note 2 for Tom Paterson's book on LifePlanning.)
2. (p. 21) See Psalm 143:8.
3. (p. 21) *Mother Teresa*, a film by Petrie Productions, Inc., 1986. Produced and directed by Jeanette and Ann Petrie. Narration by Richard Attenborough.
4. (p. 21) Brent Curtis and John Eldredge, *The Sacred Romance* (Nashville: Thomas Nelson, 1997), 19.
5. (p. 22) Bill Thrall, Bruce McNicol, and Ken McElrath, *The Ascent of a Leader: How Ordinary Relationships Develop Extraordinary Character and Influence* (San Francisco: Jossey-Bass, 1999), 147. Copyright 1999 by Leadership Catalyst, Inc.
6. (p. 23) In a conversation with the author at Missionaries of Charity Mother House, Calcutta, India, 1 December, 1987.

Chapter 2

LEAVE YOUR PAST BEHIND

Forgetting what is behind and straining toward what is ahead,
I press on toward the goal to win the prize
for which God has called me heavenward in Christ Jesus.
(PHILIPPIANS 3:13–14)

Envision following the pathway to purpose like crossing a broad stream in the mountains. As we anticipate taking our first step together, we can already catch a glimpse of the inviting glades and inspiring vistas on the far bank. A worthy prize most certainly awaits us! Our urge might be to get there as quickly as possible, but the stream runs swift and is interspersed with deep pools. Fortunately, God has provided clearly defined stepping-stones to help us navigate safely across. So before you take your first step and risk a plunge into the chilling waters, let's pause to make sure you're ready for the journey ahead.

Take a moment to ask yourself tough questions about the pace at which you think you should proceed: *Can I handle an intense, full-speed-ahead pace right now? Am I physically, emotionally, and spiritually prepared to leave all else behind and strain ahead to fulfill some or all of God's purposes for my life? Might it be best for the time being to take a more leisurely approach? Should I press on one step at a time, no matter how slowly, or should I simply take a quick first pass through to get the "lay of the land" for a future journey?*

THE CRUCIAL FIRST STEP

If you're ready to go, let's consider the first step, which is taken from the Scripture passage at the beginning of this chapter: *forget what is behind so that we can press on toward our goal.* If this seems like an odd first step to you, let me tell you it seemed that way to me too, but God knows what he is doing. He knows that the heavy weight of the past can wear us down as if we're carrying a backpack loaded with bricks. It can keep us from winning the prize. To *forget what is behind* is actually a great gift from God to you. Let's explore why.

God's directive to forget is wonderfully freeing. To forget means to put distance between you and the troubles and sorrows you've seen. It rids you of guilt and shame, and it will lessen your load of regret or bitterness. It gives you a fresh perspective that you *did* survive sadness and that you are emotionally stronger than you previously thought. It will bring you a generous supply of hope when you understand that God has seen everything you have gone through and that he controls how to use all of it in his plan for fulfilling his purposes in your life.

Forgetting the past so that we can press on toward the future isn't an instant, one-step event; it is a multifaceted process. Psychologists tell us that we really can't forget something (except through dangerous repression of it) until we have experienced some type of healing. So before we launch full-steam ahead down the pathway to purpose, we need to allow healing to be a legitimate life focus for a period of time. It really is okay to give yourself permission to slow your pursuit of purpose in order to concentrate on healing and to put behind you whatever could overwhelm or immobilize you on the journey ahead.

> *Those who are able to honestly and courageously deal with the past as a learning and shaping tool will take the road that leads to authentic living. That's a way of life that enables us to honestly accept ourselves for who we are — warts, weaknesses, and all.*[1]
> DR. JOHN TRENT

If at this time you have some nasty, old, relational wounds that are still open, or if your emotions are raw because your world recently has been turned upside down, you may need to proceed cautiously on this exploration into the unknown, but *do* proceed. With the help of the Holy Spirit, face the heartache, grief, or trauma that is tearing you apart. This chapter will get you started. You don't need to worry about the steps that will follow. Healing is your top-priority purpose for your life today.

THE HAZARDS OF SKIPPING THIS STEP

You may be tempted to skip the step of healing and putting the past behind. You may consider it to be less important than what God *really* wants you to do for him. If that is your response, beware. You could set yourself up for a vicious cycle of unlearned lessons, unsolved issues, and unresolved grief. You won't be psychologically, emotionally, or spiritually equipped to handle any big, new assignments from God. I know, because that's exactly what I did.

When I was younger, I failed to realize that it was necessary to recognize, deal with, and heal from the past so I put it behind me. I thought I could simply ignore it and go on. I was an expert mimic of Scarlett O'Hara's method of dealing with reality in *Gone With the Wind*. Her words, "I'll think about that tomorrow," sounded like a good idea to me.

Even as a newlywed, the pain of life and my denial began taking its toll. My husband Gary was a young, dynamic police detective who was awarded the Medal of Valor for risking his life to save a fellow officer. The plaque he received read, in part: "With total disregard for his own safety, for personal heroism above and beyond the call of duty, for extraordinary bravery in the face of imminent physical danger. . . ." While Gary felt deeply honored to have been of service to the police force, a part of me died of fright. But I dutifully buried the feelings of worry and fear deep within and began my survival trek.

I learned how to stay calm in my husband's world of cops and robbers, and later, undercover narcotics work. My coping motto seemed ingenious to me: *I am Super Wife of Super Cop. I can handle anything.* That was not a sophisticated or scriptural approach to stress, but I was young and had no idea I was setting myself up for a fall.

Then, in 1981, at age thirty-four, Gary had a heart attack while on duty. That shock was followed by triple bypass surgery and forced retirement from the police department. In his mind, Gary had gone from hero to has-been in seven short years. We faced more than unemployment and income issues. We were stunned by the abrupt loss of his lifelong dream of being a great cop, which everyone knew was one of his deepest passions.

To make matters worse, one of his surgeons told him, "You'll probably have to be cracked open again in five years." So I watched my husband become a textbook case of someone suffering from the fear of dying. My specialty became cheerleading. I felt it was my job to put on a happy face and hold it all together.

But our lives were out of control. The year following Gary's heart attack was one crisis after another. One of my best friends, a fellow instructor at the community college where I taught, died, as did one of my favorite students. My father-in-law and mother were both in and out of the hospital with heart problems. Our home flooded with two feet of water. In the midst of it all, we made numerous emergency trips to the hospital. I vividly remember standing alone in the hospital late one night, shaking, while the doctors used chest paddles to bring my husband back after his heart stopped. I hadn't even had time to call our families. And just to make things a little more interesting, I became pregnant with our second child. But no matter what happened, I managed everything because that's what I was supposed to do.

I didn't do well after the birth of our gorgeous, healthy baby girl, however. Due to an undiagnosed thyroid condition, my hormones dragged me into a deep depression that lasted well beyond the normal postpartum blues. For five months I did little but sit in my recliner wrapped in my pink bathrobe, sleeping and crying. Some days I couldn't even get out of bed.

I wrote in my journal that I was living a nightmare, that I had slipped into a bottomless hole in the center of the earth from which I couldn't escape. At times, I couldn't even write. I could only stare, numb and broken, at the second hand on the clock and beg, "God, if you have any compassion left for me, get me through the next second."

I asked my family and friends to pray for me because I was so low I couldn't pray. I felt like a porcelain doll ready to shatter into a thousand pieces. At one point I scribbled on the back of an envelope of an overdue bill:

Swirling down through pitch darkness into a bottomless, black abyss. Enormously sad, afraid, and confused. Sitting in the dark. Exhausted and without hope.

Later, during my slow recovery I wrote,

Lord, I know positively that I cannot survive another hell-on-earth experience. I will never again have the behemoth strength that it would take to cooperate with you bringing me back from the dead a second time. If a serious depression recurs, I need you to know that I would rather stay dead emotionally or just die physically. This has been the saddest and hardest ordeal of my life.

I'd like to say that quickly thereafter I took appropriate steps to forget the despair of my past and put it all behind me, but I didn't. Instead, I learned the art of living in manic mode. I was good at it, and as time passed, I got better at it.

During the years following our divorce, I purchased a brand-new red convertible, hired a personal shopper, put a swimming pool in my backyard, puttered around the world, got advanced degrees, and learned to play hardball at a corporate job. My coping strategy became, "If you spend enough, travel enough, work enough, and become enough of a perfectionist, it numbs the pain." I avoided hurt because I was terrified that feeling it would plunge me into another depression.

God specializes in taking the "weaklings" of the world and turning them into strong beautiful souls. In his eyes, brokenness is not a failure; it is the gateway to a deeper spirituality.[2]
JUDITH COUCHMAN

Besides, a single mother in manic mode *moves;* she gets things done whereas a depressed mom doesn't.

It seems amazing to me now, but I actually thought I could find God's purpose in the midst of my frantic life! It didn't occur to me that numbing the pain had become my purpose. I had no idea how much the weight of my past influenced my life every day. It took years for me to hear God's voice calling out to me through the noise and confusion in which I lived.

As we continue our journey on the pathway to purpose, I will share more of how I slowly began to forget the past and press on toward the goal for which Christ had called me. But for now, please understand that I am a poster child of God's grace. I never imagined that God could or would use a wreck like me to minister to other women. The thought of it is still incomprehensible, but God is doing it, and I will be forever grateful and humbled.

NO MATTER HOW DARK THE PAST, YOU CAN PRESS ON

I love the way God takes any and all willing Christians—no matter how broken or scarred their past—and weaves every thread of their lives into his kingdom-building plan. He doesn't shy away from our hurts or failures, but specializes in hope, second chances, and resurrections. He's present with you right now, equipping you and nudging you to prepare yourself to do his work on earth.

I have mentored and grown to love some gutsy women who have survived horrific problems and sadness. They are real women who, at one time or another, have been in desperate need of hope. They have faced the past, put it in the hands of their Lord, and pressed forward. Although some of them are famous or wealthy or accomplished in their fields, what impresses me about them are their incredible testimonies of hardship, brokenness, and renewal.

One is a grandmother whose precious two-year-old granddaughter died of AIDS after receiving a blood transfusion. Another is a woman whose husband left his wedding ring and a one-sentence note on the nightstand: "I can't be married to you any longer." When one friend was a newly licensed teenage driver, she accidentally backed a car over her toddler sister, killing her. Another is a mother who held her son's split skull together while waiting for an ambulance to arrive at the scene of their remote automobile accident.

These women have braved the agony of life, and they know how God can use such experiences to bring good out of bad. They have visited the depths of hell and have lived to proclaim to others that God never left their side for a second. They have witnessed his power and grace, even among their scattered ashes of hopelessness. May you find comfort in knowing that if God can find ways to use their pain and mine to accomplish his purposes, he can use yours too.

> *I still have bad days, but that's okay. I used to have bad years.*
> ANONYMOUS

SO WHAT ABOUT YOUR LIFE?

You may have had relatively little sorrow in your life, or you may have endured dreadful experiences. Life may be tough for you *today*:

- You may be in a constant battle with the *annoying* things of life, like a demanding boss or strange, expensive noises in your car.
- Perhaps the *chronic* things in life threaten to overwhelm you: disciplining a belligerent teenager, praying for an unsaved husband, caring for a disabled child, or facing your own fears.
- Perhaps you encounter the *unexpected* things: the phone call from your mother-in-law asking if she can move in, or your doctor's voice saying "I'm sorry; it's malignant," or a letter

from the IRS demanding payment on some back taxes, or a note from your daughter saying she's no longer able to raise her children so she's left them in front of your television set.

   ❦ Your battles may be against the *sinful* things in life such as adultery, addiction, or aggression.

   ❦ Your challenge may be dealing with the *unspeakable* things such as haunting memories of abuse or the disappearance of your child.

You may not have a clue as to how you could ever forget your past or present crises, let alone press on. Even reading that God wants you to do so may be upsetting to you. But please, no matter what your past or present circumstances, hang on to the hope that God is with you.

Your past and present, not only the bad things that have happened to you but also the good things—your successes, relationships, hopes, longings, morals, motives, spiritual beliefs, self-esteem, and personality—have shaped who you are today. God has chosen to use every part of you in his plan: your mind, body, and soul, your past and your present. He does not need a shoehorn to squeeze his plan into your life circumstances. He is able to move effortlessly.

You keep track of all my sorrows.

You have collected all my tears in your bottle.

You have recorded each one in your book.
(Psalm 56:8, NLT)

Are you willing to empty your backpack of its load of bricks? Are you willing to unload the excess weight of your past and let old wounds heal? Then let's press on. God wants you to get to the other side of the stream for your own sake, so that someday you can come back and help others find their way across.

The Sojourner's Guide to "Unpacking" the Past

The following suggestions and activities are designed to help you put the past behind you and press on toward discovering God's purpose for your life. Take whatever time you need to complete each step, and resist the temptation to take shortcuts. On this journey, shortcuts lead only to dead ends!

Write about Your Pain

After a time of prayer during which you ask God to guide you, write down the negative elements of your past, especially your most painful memories. (The *Pathway to Purpose for Women Personal Journal*, or any journal or notebook, would be a helpful tool to record information such as this.) Regardless of how long ago a hurtful experience occurred, if you are still struggling with the fallout, you must deal with it in order to be prepared to accomplish God's purposes for your life. Processing your grief or pain is not negotiable. Tell God that you want to let go of the concerns of your past and that you want him to take those experiences from you and help you forget them.

If someone whom you need to forgive or from whom you need to ask forgiveness was involved in an incident, do all you can to mend the relationship so you can move on. Bringing closure to the problem will help you heal. As you work at your own pace through each memory, cross it off the list.

A WORD OF CAUTION: If you are struggling through grief or depression, or have deep wounds from your past, you may need professional help to face and process those issues. Start by admitting the hurt to yourself. Then choose a wise confidante such as a pastor, church leader, counselor, or mature friend to help you move toward healing.

Recall a Time You Healed

Think of an emotional or physical hurt from which you have already healed. Imagine that healing process as if it were a section of rough terrain you faced, perhaps a mountain you climbed or a canyon you bridged. Do you remember how daunting the whole ordeal was? Can you recall how God equipped you for that journey? The fact that you made it through is evidence of his power at work in you. Look back at the view you now have from this side of the pain. Be encouraged by how far you've come.

Now, repeat the same exercise with some emotional hurt you would like to see healed. Envision the challenge you face, then imagine the victory God will give you. Don't let the arduous process bother you, because you've already traversed similar territory. God has helped you survive before. Let him do it for you again.

Prayerfully Decide to Trust God

Decide today to trust that God has a plan to use your past for good in the future. This pivotal decision requires an act of your will. You have to *want* to make the choice to focus forward.

Write Your Testimony

If you have not already done so, write your testimony in approximately three to four pages. As you do that, you'll notice whether you are making progress in your emotional healing. Having trouble getting started? Write one page to describe what happened in your life before you knew Christ or matured in your faith, another page to describe God's mercy and how he healed you, and another page to share your insights about God's purposes for your life right now. Then remember that a testimony is a public declaration. Share it with someone!

Ask: To Whom Will My Hurt Give Hope?

I'm sure you have realized by now that ministering to others in the field of life purpose education resonates with a deep ache in my soul. God ministered to me in a profound way when I understood that he was using my past, including my heartaches in the area of purposelessness, to help others. Seeing the heavy burdens and needs of others hungry to know the truth about God's plan for their lives freed me from my emotional paralysis, victim mentality, and negative thinking.

So I urge you to identify the type of person for whom you have great empathy, one who might benefit from hearing about your hardships and hope. Ask yourself: "Which person or group of people need to know that God has promised incredible life purposes?" Then, every time you want to abandon your work of personal healing, remember the people who could eventually benefit from your continued journey.

Surround Yourself with People of Hope

Positive role models can be a powerful influence in our lives, and there are a number of ways to surround yourself with such people. Seek out someone with whom you would like to spend time and dare to ask for a meeting. Also, collect and read testimonies of people such as Corrie ten Boom, Catherine Marshall, Hannah Whitall Smith, Elisabeth Elliot, Joni Eareckson Tada, and Ruth Graham (daughter of Ruth and Billy Graham). Their stories will renew your courage and refresh your hope.

RECOMMENDED BOOKS ON HOPE AMIDST HARDSHIP

The God I Love, by Joni Eareckson Tada[3]
In Every Pew Sits a Broken Heart, by Ruth Graham[4]

NOW IS THE TIME TO TRUST IN GOD'S PURPOSES FOR YOUR LIFE

Are you ready to take this step in your life: to *forget what is behind and press on toward the goal*? If so, pursue God and his purposes for your life as you use the exercises I have outlined for you in this chapter. Take a last look at your past. Now turn your focus away and look toward the other side of the stream. You *can* press on toward the goal to win the prize for which God has called you heavenward in Christ Jesus.

God's pleasure is to make good out of bad. He is your loving and generous Father. He has a way of delicately wrapping all the parts of your life together as a package deal to give you hope and purpose. Whether tragedy has torn up your life or whether you have lived in bliss, all that matters now is that you decide to allow God to do with you as he wishes. Trust that he will use the best and worst of your past (and present too) to fulfill his purposes for your life.

This first decision as you stand on the bank of the pathway to purpose is to choose how you will respond to God's offer to use the rich soil of your life. He's waiting to hear from you. Are you ready to be God's woman of purpose, a woman of hope? Don't wait any longer. An eventful journey lies ahead.

GOD'S WISDOM FOR THE PATHWAY

THE "MARY MAGDALENE" STEP OF LIFE: FORGET WHAT IS BEHIND AND PRESS ON TOWARD THE GOAL

For a lesson from Mary Magdalene, a repentant sinner, read Luke 8:2 and John 20:1–18. Jesus had driven seven demons out of Mary Magdalene, yet she was the first person he chose to talk to after his resurrection and the one he then asked to carry a message to his disciples. Her story of God's mercy has been told for centuries as an encouragement to billions around the world. Will you let God use your life of pain, grief, problems, failure, and forgiven sin? Are you willing to let your past *demons*, delays, distrust, and destroyed dreams give hope to someone else? If yes, tell him so today.

Personal Pathway Questions

1. List five things that have caused you grief, pain, hurt, rejection, or failure (for example: cancer, sexual abuse, bankruptcy, adultery, infertility, miscarriage, abortion, death of a loved one, unemployment, theft, prejudice, natural disaster).

2. How has God used one or more of these things for good in your life?

3. Even though this chapter primarily focused on things you may want to forget and leave behind, God can also use your successes or happy memories in his plan for your life. List five such things (for example: saving money for your kid's college education, healing a broken relationship, nurturing a solid marriage, raising moral children, completing a race, overcoming an addiction, getting a bonus, buying a home, seeing the world, teaching a new believer about Christ).

4. How has God used one or more of these things for good in your life?

5. How could a combination of things on your lists be used to give hope to someone else?

NOTES

1. (p. 30) Reprinted from *LifeMapping*. Copyright 1998 by John Trent, Ph.D., WaterBrook Press, Colorado Springs, Colorado. All rights reserved.

2. (p. 34) Judith Couchman, *Designing a Woman's Life: A Bible Study and Workbook* (Sisters, Ore.: Multnomah, 1996), 91.

3. (p. 39) Joni Eareckson Tada, *The God I Love* (Grand Rapids: Zondervan, 2003).

4. (p. 39) Ruth Graham, *In Every Pew Sits a Broken Heart* (Grand Rapids: Zondervan, 2004).

Part Two

Never Walk Alone

God's *Fellowship* Purpose for You:
To Connect with Others

Chapter 3

Do What Matters Today

"As you sent me into the world,
I am sending them into the world."
(JOHN 17:18, NLT)

If you've decided to move forward on the pathway to purpose, then we're on our way! Let's take a deep breath and step out across the water to the first stepping-stone before us. Yes! That's the one. I know it is rather plain looking and not very inviting, but the stepping-stone of learning to *do today what God sent you into the world to do* is firmly embedded in the stream. This solid stone will move you one giant step farther on the pathway to purpose. But I must warn you, many women struggle on this step.

Some women stumble because they try to hop over this stepping-stone in their rush to pursue a more magnificent, profound purpose. This is particularly true of women whose lives are difficult. Their daily roles are such an arduous, unapplauded battle that they just want to shake their fist and shout to the heavens: "Enough! I want to do the fun, rewarding stuff—now!" They may be too worn out to see that today's pressing roles are already brimming with a purpose that brings glory to their Creator. They don't realize that their day-in, day-out efforts are extremely precious to the heart of God.

This is a monumental step for other women because they are skeptical. They can't see how such an unimpressive stepping-stone can lead to a grand-scale life purpose. They think, *How can there be a connection between the way I manage my routine, unglamorous, daily tasks and an exciting, larger-than-life purpose later on? How can handling the "today" things guarantee a more stimulating and purposeful tomorrow?* They don't want to be disappointed by false expectations, so they turn back toward home. Ironically, by hightailing it out of the stream they give up on their dreams, passions, longings, and hopes.

I know that the mundane responsibilities of today may seem impossibly far away from the glorious purpose you long for. I know that just doing what is before you to do today may not be very appealing. But please, plant your feet firmly on this stepping-stone. You see, there *is* a strong connection between going today where you have been sent today—no matter how difficult, incomprehensible, or unrewarding it may be—and a future, take-your-breath-away assignment from God. Fulfilling your roles today, although those roles may not be thrilling or sensational, is the safest, most predictable step you could possibly take toward tomorrow's intriguing purpose.

GOD VALUES TODAY

God has chosen a series of specific, daily tasks for each of us, and we accomplish those through our roles in our family, church, vocation, and community. He also asks us to handle the tasks-at-hand in our personal life (including our mental, physical, emotional, and spiritual well-being). Although we may not see the value in these common requirements, God is committed to using them to accomplish his purposes. So we must learn to trust him as the sovereign Lord of our "todays." Instead of asking, "What remarkable task do I want to tackle for God?" a better question is, "What does God want me to be and do in my routine world today?"

It truly is sad when a woman does not accept her most obvious life purposes as a gift from God. I say that because I am fully aware of how guilty I am of being the kettle that calls the pot black! For years I had a terrible time of it. I was always thinking I was *supposed* to be doing something else. I succumbed to viewing diaper changes and meal preparation as dull, monotonous duties rather than God-given appointments to bless those around me. During my momma-ing years I begged for a meaningful, heroic role and missed out on the purposefulness of what was before me every single day.

> *Whatever our season of life, it offers its own opportunities and challenges for spiritual growth. Instead of wishing we were in another season, we ought to find out what this one offers.*[1]
> JOHN ORTBERG

I now realize that all of our life experiences have value to God. Every day he considers our willingness and faithfulness in the ordinary things to see if we can handle the challenging, unique assignments that he loves to entrust to those who are faithful. It is not God's plan for you to spend today chasing after your future *one thing* when your *many things* are right in front of you. You were born to make a Christlike difference in hundreds of ordinary ways, not to ignore or avoid the present opportunities while looking for a bigger, more noticeable project. As my dad says so well, "Kids, just follow your script today."

Despite the relentless tedium of life's ordinary tasks, there are wonderful blessings to be found in doing today what God has sent you into the world to do. How I wish I had had the maturity years ago to grasp that God had assigned me a purpose for each day. What if I had known that he loves to honor the obedience of his everyday, ordinary women who serve him tirelessly (even when they're tired)? It would have been encouraging to realize that God saw and would reward the daily roles of servanthood into which I was pouring my life. It would have been comforting to realize that those efforts mattered to him. What a lifeline to hope I could have held on to if I had known that those experiences were part of his plan to prepare my character and faith so that he could entrust me with a greater responsibility in the future.

Jesus sheds light on another generous bonus gift God gives when we take this step. Read his words recorded in John 17:17–18: "Make them pure and holy by teaching them your words of truth. As you sent me into the world, I am sending them into the world" (NLT). In this prayer, Jesus asks God, his Father, to sanctify (set apart) his followers to do his Father's will in the world today by helping them believe and obey the truth of the Word of God. Jesus knows we won't be able to value our roles through our own efforts. Only applying God's Word to our everyday, routine circumstances can purify both heart and mind. God's Word reveals sin, motivates us to forgive, causes us to repent, and helps us desire to be pure and holy, like Christ. It consecrates us for our day-to-day roles and God's future goals for us in the world.

Once you realize the great importance of your "ordinary" roles in God's eyes, you will understand that you're in over your head! You will recognize the many ways in which you are not like Christ. You will see your limits. That will cause you to run to God for help. You will know that in order to be genuinely on-task in your unremittingly demanding world, you must always be focused on God's great, eternal purpose to make you like Christ. You will discover that you need to live in partnership with Jesus Christ. You will desire to worship the only one who can see you through the daily challenges you face.

> *Then they answered Joshua: "Whatever you have commanded us we will do, and wherever you send us we will go."*
> (JOSHUA 1:16)

Once we begin to appreciate the treasure of today's roles, we begin to experience the stress-reducing benefits of peace and rest. Once we believe that God values our today, we can stop looking for the greener pastures of more grandiose or broad-reach assignments. We can let go of all the things people say we should be doing. We can rest in the knowledge that every day (yes, every task) is locked safely in God's heart. We can hold on to the dreams God has given us about the future without the pressure of having to make them happen right this second!

So, What about *Your* Roles?

Now that we understand a bit of how God views our everyday roles, let's take a closer look at the roles you are presently filling. Are you a daughter, sister, aunt, niece, cousin, spouse, mother, grandmother, boss, employee, friend, neighbor, student, community volunteer, and/or lay minister?

Do you realize that each one of these commitments makes you a valuable missionary for Christ? A missionary is "a person sent to do religious or charitable work in some territory."[2] Your work as God's missionary takes place in a specific location—a home, church, office, school, neighborhood, state, or nation. Your assignment, done through the love of Jesus in conjunction with and for the benefit of others, touches any immediate circumstance in which you are involved— whether that is playing a board game with your kids, volunteering at a school, running for mayor, acting in community theater, dating, or lobbying in Washington. How would you evaluate your current "missionary status"? Are you happy or joyful about it? Or, is it a struggle for you to see real value in it? If it's a struggle, you have plenty of company.

I, for one, had a hard time appraising the spiritual value and merit of my mothering years. For example, when I took my children, and often an entire crew of neighborhood kids, on outings to the zoo, park, beach, or fire department, I had the feeling that I was playing, not accomplishing something of value. When I read to my kids, played hide-and-seek, or drew

> *Have you identified your mission? Usually there are many places to live out your mission: your mission as a spouse or parent or child, as a Christian, as a neighbor, as an employee, as a friend.*[3]
> Jane Kise,
> David Stark, and
> Sandra Hirsh

pictures with them, I felt guilty for goofing off. When I planned their birthday parties, took them to the dentist, walked them to the bus stop, or helped them with homework, I didn't think what I was doing counted for much because I wasn't producing anything of measurable value.

At the time, I couldn't see the total picture. Sometimes I wondered, *Does how hard I work today or how well I cope even matter in the greater scheme of things?* At other times I equated significance with mega-effort. My frustration often turned into a cruel, personal scrutiny of everything I did.

> *There's a time when you have to explain to your children why they're born, and it's a marvelous thing if you know the reason by then.*[4]
> HAZEL SCOTT,
> AMERICAN–WEST
> INDIAN PIANIST

It wasn't until years later that I discovered my parenting efforts were of real value. I now understand that the investment I made in my children's lives did (and does) matter. Parenting isn't just my responsibility, it is one of my God-ordained roles in life. Knowing that I am on-target with them has allowed me to taste meaning in the present, ordinary moments. What a relief! Today I enjoy those moments to the fullest. My favorite things are sharing an uninterrupted meal with my son and his wife or relaxing and listening to my daughter sing.

If you are a mom, I encourage you to be grateful for the high calling God has given you today. Motherhood is an anointed role. Don't beg for distractions. Instead, immerse yourself in the experiences of today. Value them and make the most of them. At the right time, God will lead you onward, and you will be able to see the importance of today's ordinary tasks in the total scope of God's purposes.

Of course, moms are not the only women who may feel out of place, frustrated, or confused in their present roles. Lori, for example, is a single professional woman with an excellent job. Her superb administrative skills fit well with her responsibilities of coordinating projects with a creative production team and participating in high-level meetings within her organization. Her personal values mesh well with those of her coworkers. Yet Lori feels "stuck" and wonders if her life dreams will die from neglect. She often feels as if she is just "marking time" in her present job when she truly longs to make a significant, full-time contribution in the lives of elderly people in her community.

No matter what your current roles in life may be, let me assure you that God will use them for good in the future. He saw me through tough times as a single mom, a career woman, an entrepreneur, and a housekeeper for others. In fact, God was always molding me in each of those situations, even though I could not rise above the exhausting repetition and endless to-do lists of my roles at the time.

WHEN IT'S HARD TO SEE THE PURPOSE

It is one thing to realize that God has ordained many mini-purposes in even the most ordinary days of our lives. It is quite another to live it. At times, no matter how committed we are to seeking God's purpose in the day-to-day grind, the grind ultimately wears us down. What do we do then? What exactly is God up to when life is out of control for us? What are we to think when stress seems to knock us down at every turn?

Let me share more of my story, and you may relate to some of the uncertainty and confusion I experienced during a particularly difficult time. It began in 1990, when my ex-husband had quadruple bypass surgery this time and died several days later. I was stunned. He had been an angel of a father and a gentleman of an "ex" (I know that sounds like an oxymoron, but it was absolutely true).

Nothing in my life has ever compared to the heavy responsibility of telling my children that their daddy was not coming home—ever—that he had gone to heaven to be with Jesus. As I sat in the principal's office at my children's school, disoriented, waiting for my third-grade daughter and fifth-grade son to be called out of their classrooms, I wondered what I could say to tell them how sorry I was. How could I fully communicate my concern for their heartache of being fatherless when I hadn't ever experienced that myself?

I decided it would be best to wait three months before I let myself grieve deeply so that I could be more emotionally available to my kids. Earlier than I anticipated, however, and without my permission, a moderate depression began hanging around me like a dark storm cloud. I struggled to understand how such dark days could serve any good purpose. In due time, I knew I had to take appropriate steps to move on so that depression would not incapacitate me.

Just one year after my ex-husband's death, I was laid off from my job due to a corporate reorganization. Although company managers were sympathetic and ever-so-careful with my feelings when they delivered the awful news, my dazed mind heard: *Faithful and loyal employee, you're fired! Go home! Here is your severance check and the telephone number of your new best friend, your outplacement counselor.* I wanted to scream back, "I'll go home when I'm good and ready!"

The loss of my job shook my world because by then I was the sole support for my children. In addition, I had foolishly purchased a new home a few months prior without having sold my other residence. I had gambled with fate that our old house would sell quickly and of course had not anticipated the notorious call from Human Resources. Unfortunately, I couldn't just take back the house to a customer service counter and say, "I'd like to return this. I already have one of these."

> *Be true to the grief and feelings until they're all played out. There is no formula.*[5]
> STANLEE PHELPS, EXECUTIVE OUTPLACEMENT COUNSELOR AND MY "NEW BEST FRIEND"

The job loss renewed the troubling questions about what my purpose in life really was. It was also tough on my ego because my job had been a cushy, executive public relations job. I had been schmoozing for a living. A long day for me might include approving layouts for an annual stockholders' report, flying by helicopter to attend a CEO luncheon with the chairman of the board, and entertaining constituents at a ballet later that evening.

To make matters worse, my job was eliminated eighteen days before Christmas, which happens to be the anniversary of the bombing of Pearl Harbor. I felt like my little *career island* had been bombed while I was supposed to be saying, "Merry Christmas, kids!"

If you have struggled through similar adversities, you know that the real challenge is that problems such as these can feel as if they'll never end. Of course you know that circumstances do eventually shift, but it is hard to see the end of the trial when you are going through it. It is even harder to see the purpose or meaning in it.

During the fourteen long months when I did not have a professional job, the unending monotony of some of my basic chores like house-cleaning and cooking really got to me. I have to agree with comedian Phyllis Diller who has said, "Cleaning your house while your kids are still growing is like shoveling the walk before it stops snowing." Just what was the point? I wanted to accomplish something with my life!

In Hindsight

Several years later, the pressures of life began to let up a little. I nestled into a fairly stable time when I was better able to reflect on God's agenda through each of my complicated situations. My actual life purposes were still no clearer to me than pieces of an unframed jigsaw puzzle, but I could begin to see a vague picture on the box. That image assured me that God had a plan and it gave me hope.

In hindsight, I see that God had given me a variety of important assignments during the entire twenty-year period of my life that I've just sketched out for you. My first and foremost purpose was to get to know God intimately and to learn that I had value because he created me, not because of what I could do. My secondary purpose was to be a good wife and mother, helping to raise our son and daughter as godly people. In addition, I was called upon to be a good daughter, sister, relative, friend, employee, church member and volunteer, neighbor, and graduate student.

Little did I suspect that God had assigned a distinct purpose in each of my roles and life events. I never imagined that my tough experiences were giving me the substance I would later need to minister to others. I never guessed that God was intent on sculpting into my character traits like humility, faithfulness, patience, and mercy. I had no idea that those maturing years were preparing me to offer the same hope to other women that God provided for me as he pulled me through each day.

Was I ready to hear from God about a far-reaching, high-impact assignment years ago? Although I thought I was at the time, the answer was "No, of course not!" I now know that the most important stuff that happens in life is often challenging, rarely exhilarating, and frequently frightening. I am so grateful that God never wastes a hurt. He uses them all to prepare our heart, mind, body, and soul to receive and worship him. Through the day-to-day grind I began to gain the wisdom and strength to live out the big purposes of life hand-in-hand with God. I began to look forward to the same blessing the prophet Jeremiah wrote about:

> But blessed is the [wo]man who trusts in the Lord and has made the Lord [her] hope and confidence. [She] is like a tree planted along a riverbank, with its roots reaching deep into the water—a tree not bothered by the heat nor worried by long months of drought. Its leaves stay green, and it goes right on producing all its luscious fruit.[6]

God used my grief, my battle with depression, and my job loss to allow me to empathize with women in whom discouragement and despair are running rampant, with women who have been through everyday craziness or appalling crises. What a privilege it is for me to comfort them while they discern, prioritize, appreciate, and balance the work God has scheduled for them to do today and in the future. How blessed and useful I feel when I help a woman save time and tears. Who but God could have orchestrated such goodness and purpose out of my painful yesterdays?

No matter what your life roles, whether you are a widowed grandmother, divorced waitress, dedicated cancer researcher, underpaid missionary, retired flight attendant, depressed graduate student, never-been-married parole officer, or unappreciated carpool driver, listen to God's instructions for your life. Although you may wish he had stamped your forehead with your current and future purposes, God knows you're smarter than that. He wants you to heed the apostle Paul's counsel: "Since we live by the Spirit, let us keep in step with the Spirit."[7] He expects you to travel through life fulfilling your individual, daily purposes, guided by the Holy Spirit who will direct your steps.

> *It's like a man going away: He leaves his house and puts his servants in charge, each with his assigned task.*
> (MARK 13:34)

I believe that even in the midst of your ordinary routine, God reveals hints about what he's called you to do. The Bible tells us that "God has given each of you some special abilities; be sure to use them to help each other,"[8] so God has already blessed you with spiritual gifts, skills, talents, and natural abilities. Whether you are able to teach, lead, feed, draw, sing, build, analyze, research, motivate, organize, write, or something else, God will provide situations to use those gifts to further his kingdom. That's why Scripture admonishes us to use our gifts in accordance with the grace God has given us.[9]

Your daily roles are incredible opportunities for you to use your natural and spiritual giftedness to help your family, friends, and neighbors learn about and become more like Christ. God breathed those traits into you purposefully to help you share his message in your everyday world. When you dedicate your heart and giftedness to work in concert with God's current roles for your life, you may even begin to hear yourself say, "Life is good. I've never had such a sense of fulfillment. Thank you, Lord, for giving me such important tasks. How have I found such favor with you?"

PURPOSE-FILLED WOMEN OF THE BIBLE

God breathed purpose into the lives of women we read about in the Bible. I have often wondered if they could possibly have known the importance of their incredible life assignments. I'm now convinced that they were just showing up for work and being obedient to wherever God placed them on any given day. Some of them had assignments in their home, workplace, congregation, or community. As you read more about them, consider what their faithful surrender to God's will for their lives accomplished.

Mary, the mother of Jesus, joined other women in the first recorded prayer meeting.[10]

Anna, a prophetess, was the first witness to the Jews.[11]

Mary Magdalene was last at the cross,[12] first at the tomb,[13] and first to proclaim the Resurrection.[14]

Lydia, a businesswoman, was the first to greet the Christian missionaries, Paul and Silas, in Europe, and she was the first convert on that continent.[15]

Mary of Bethany was honored by Christ.[16]

Deborah was a judge.[17]

Ruth was a faithful, enterprising daughter-in-law.[18]

Hannah was the mother of Samuel.[19]

Abigail has become known as the first female public relations official.[20]

The Shunammite woman was a hospitable friend to Elisha.[21]

Elizabeth was the mother of John the Baptist.[22]

Joanna was a traveling helpmate for Jesus.[23]

Susanna was a financial supporter of Jesus and his disciples.[24]

The Samaritan woman at the well is now called an evangelist.[25]

Dorcas was a benevolent seamstress and church leader.[26]

Phoebe was a servant of the church.[27]

Priscilla was a fellow worker with Paul.[28]

Rahab was a prostitute, but showed faith in God when she welcomed the Israelite spies into Jericho.[29]

THE SOJOURNER'S GUIDE
TO DOING WHAT MATTERS TODAY

The following suggestions are designed to help you begin fulfilling your purposes for today so that you can press on toward discovering God's ultimate purpose for your life. Take whatever time you need to process these, and resist the temptation to take shortcuts!

Prioritize Your Roles

It is hard to find purpose if we're unclear about our priorities. So take the time to consider your most important roles and prioritize them in your mind, heart, and schedule. Make a commitment today to live by this list as much as possible:

- What is my most important role in life?

- What is my second most important role in life?

- What is my third most important role in life?

- What is my fourth most important role in life?

- What is my fifth most important role in life?

Take Good Care of Yourself

If you are going to go the distance for God, you must take care of the physical temple in which you live. Ask yourself: "Am I exercising, eating right, getting enough rest, drinking enough water, and enjoying laughter breaks?" If not, what three things will you do to improve your self-care during the next thirty days?

Don't Panic

Life is not fair. We live in a fallen world. Tough times are inevitable. But don't panic! Even God's highest purposes can be extremely difficult or utterly exhausting for a time. Think about it for a moment. What higher purpose could there be for a woman than caring for a terminally ill family member? Yet a great deal of sorrow goes along with fulfilling such an all-consuming role.

No matter what roles you fulfill or difficulties you face, please realize that God will not abandon you. He will be right there with you. Rely on him to help you through. What role or task presses your panic button? How can you depend on God to be your strength in that situation?

Seize the Moment

Don't miss the daily parade of life by looking for the circus tent and magic show! What "parades" do you tend to miss? Think of what you can do to seize the moments before you.

RECOMMENDED BOOKS ON LIFE ROLES

Professionalizing Motherhood, by Jill Savage[30]
The Search for Significance, by Robert McGee[31]

NOW IS THE TIME TO DO WHAT MATTERS TODAY

God is not trying to hide his will from you. He wants to use where he has placed you today to prepare you for tomorrow. It is your responsibility to focus on your roles with conscientious care and to watch for God's strategically placed road signs of where to turn. He wants to reveal his plan to you as you read, study, and meditate on his Word, as well as when you pray, listen to sermons, and converse with other Christians. He is available to guide you step-by-step along the path he has set for you, if you will take time to seek his direction. So, will you take this next step toward God and his purpose for your life? Will you *do today what God sent you into the world to do?*

Please understand that a few women will perceive the miracle in which they participated only in retrospect. They will not know the role they played in history until after the fact. I can't tell you why God orchestrates such stealth missions. They are not the norm, but they do occur.

But, if you are like most women who are faithful in their day-to-day roles, a moment will come when the telephone will ring, your pager will beep, a letter or email will arrive, someone will knock on the door, or God will use some other method to deliver his ultimate vision for your life. When God decides to enlarge your current, daily roles or open your eyes to a broad-reach vision, your heart will skip a few beats. But don't worry! You don't need to call the paramedics! That's a normal response to taking a giant step forward.

GOD'S WISDOM FOR THE PATHWAY

THE "LYDIA" STEP OF LIFE: DO TODAY WHAT GOD SENT YOU INTO THE WORLD TO DO

For a lesson about how to embrace your current roles in life, read Acts 16:11-15, 40 about Lydia. She was a successful businesswoman widely known in cities near and far for selling dyed purple cloth and dyed goods to many households, including those of royalty. In addition, she was a worshiper of God. After she heard Paul preach, she was baptized and became the first convert to Christianity in all of Europe! Lydia then opened her home to Paul and the other new disciples of Jesus in that place. Are you, like Lydia, embracing your everyday assignments in life, whether that is as a household engineer, career woman, ministry leader, or other?

Personal Pathway Questions

1. You fill many roles in your circle of intimacy and sphere of influence. Write a brief, creative description of who you are in some of those roles. I wrote the paragraph below about my own life to give you an example. Have fun with the exercise!

Who am I?

I'm a maturing Christian who has good days and bad days. A daughter who is learning how to bond with my dad, now that my mom has died. A good sister to my seven siblings, an accountability partner, and prayer warrior. An aunt who takes my twenty incredible nieces and nephews for granted, as if they'll always be the wonderful ages they are now. A best friend to a few women. An introvert who must balance relationships with solitude. A shy and private neighbor, a swimmer, and a seminary student. An entrepreneur, who is proud to have failed at least a half dozen times. An ex-wife who made complete amends with my "ex." A church staff member, author, and speaker. A single mom and mother-in-law who's grateful that I'm not a grandmother yet! But, I'm not a cook, gardener, or interior designer. And, it's safe to say that I'm no longer a marathoner!

2. Write any other creative titles you may have. Here are a few to illustrate how diverse your roles may be: Family Financial Manager, Logistician, Television Cop, Keeper of Family Heritage and Traditions, Chief Cook and Bottle Washer.

3. In what way are you surprised or impressed at how many roles you're trying to fill?

NOTES

1. (p. 47) John Ortberg, *The Life You've Always Wanted* (Grand Rapids: Zondervan, 1997), 59.

2. (p. 49) William Morris, ed., *The American Dictionary of the English Language* (Boston: Houghton Mifflin, 1981), 840.

3. (p. 49) Jane Kise, David Stark, and Sandra Hirsh, *LifeKeys* (Minneapolis: Bethany House, 1996), 209.

4. (p. 50) In *The Quotable Woman: Witty, Poignant, and Insightful Observations from Notable Women* (Philadelphia: Running Press, 1991), 72.

5. (p. 52) In a conversation with the author in March 1992. Stanlee Phelps is the author of *Assertive Woman*, 3rd ed. (San Luis Obispo, Calif.: Impact, 1997). She is currently a Senior Vice President and Senior Master Coach at Lee Hecht Harrison.

6. (p. 54) Jeremiah 17:7–8, TLB.

7. (p. 55) Galatians 5:25.

8. (p. 55) 1 Peter 4:10, TLB.

9. (p. 55) See Romans 12:6.

10. (p. 56) See Acts 1:14.

11. (p. 56) See Luke 2:36–38.

12. (p. 56) See Mark 15:40–47.

13. (p. 56) See John 20:1.

14. (p. 56) See Matthew 28:1–10.

15. (p. 56) See Acts 16:13–14.

16. (p. 56) See Matthew 26:13.

17. (p. 56) See Judges 4–5.

18. (p. 56) See Ruth 1–4.

19. (p. 56) See 1 Samuel 1:20.

20. (p. 56) See 1 Samuel 25:32–35.

21. (p. 56) See 2 Kings 4:8–10.

22. (p. 56) See Luke 1:57.

23. (p. 56) See Luke 8:1–3.

24. (p. 56) See Luke 8:1–3.

25. (p. 56) See John 4:28–29.

26. (p. 56) See Acts 9:36.

27. (p. 56) See Romans 16:1–2.

28. (p. 56) See Romans 16:3.

29. (p. 56) See Hebrews 11:31.

30. (p. 58) Jill Savage, *Professionalizing Motherhood* (Grand Rapids: Zondervan, 2002).

31. (p. 58) Robert McGee, *The Search for Significance* (Nashville: W Publishing Group, 2003).

LOVE OTHERS AS JESUS LOVES YOU

"I am giving a new commandment to you now—love each other just as much as I love you. Your strong love for each other will prove to the world that you are my disciples."
(JOHN 13:34-35, TLB)

You may find the next stepping-stone on the pathway to purpose much more inviting than the previous one. This ancient, well-worn stone is *love each other as Jesus loves you.* Everyone who faithfully follows Jesus toward God's ultimate purpose eventually steps onto this stone and finds sure footing before moving forward. There is no alternate route for crossing the stream.

This step may be easier for you if you're a "relational type," but no matter what your personality, I urge you to linger on this stepping-stone for a while. Do not succumb to the temptation to lightly touch down on this stone, then skip quickly to the next one. Women who already love others or women who confess they'd rather not learn how to love are most inclined to move on prematurely.

Camp out on this stepping-stone for as long as necessary. Take whatever time you need to ensure that loving others as Jesus loves you connects permanently in your heart and mind. Loving as Jesus loves is one of your most basic life purposes. It is critical to every other life purpose God has in mind for you.

Think about it for a moment. Can you imagine that God would want you to serve others without love? How could Jesus want you to share the gospel without love? How is it possible to grow spiritually, to become more like our loving Savior, unless we also grow in love? Don't rush a good thing. Learning to love others is worth whatever investment it requires.

I'm a bit embarrassed to admit it, but I perched on this stone for six, long years! During that time I prayed that I would become a "people person." Day after day I prayed, "Lord, help me to like people." And day after day I waited. Day after day, nothing happened. Year after year, nothing happened. As you will soon discover, I was confused about what loving others really means. The good news is that God did not leave me there. He is still answering my prayer to fall madly in love with all sorts of people.

THE LESSON WE NEVER STOP LEARNING

Before we explore how to grow in love, we had better define Christlike love. How did Jesus love? How can we imitate his love? What is the love that we are called to share so freely? Does it have to do with connecting heart-to-heart with people and enjoying their company? Is it like warm fuzzies and camaraderie? Is it laughter, good times, and having fun?

While we may enjoy these rewarding experiences in loving relationships, the emotional perks of friendship and love are not the focus, nor the essence, of Christlike love. Jesus summed up the basis of love when he said, "As the Father has loved me, so have I loved you. . . . My command is this: Love each other as I have loved you. Greater love has no one than this, that he lay down his life for his friends."[1] Then Jesus did exactly that. He laid down his life for us. He gave all that he was, all that he had, to do one thing—provide the way for us to spend eternity with God. Love, then, is spending ourselves, investing ourselves, in the daily and eternal well-being of others. It is a huge calling. Are you wondering if you are willing, much less up to the challenge?

We must never forget that becoming a woman who loves others as Jesus loves is not merely a pleasant suggestion: it is a biblical mandate. Jesus gave us what he called a new *commandment* in John 13:34–35, the passage that begins this chapter. He says that our love sends a powerful message to the world around us. Our love for others gives evidence of God's love, and love is the proof of our commitment to Christ.

Loving others will always be a growth step for us. No matter how healthy or loving our relationships already are, Christ's exemplary love can always teach us more. As women who claim to be Christ's disciples, it is our calling and privilege to grow in our understanding of the extravagant, unconditional love of Jesus. It is both a challenge and an honor to intentionally strive toward that goal in every relationship and in every circumstance.

> *You will find, as you look back upon your life, that the moments when you have really lived are the moments when you have done things in the spirit of love.*
> HENRY DRUMMOND, 19TH-CENTURY EVANGELIST

When we focus on loving as Jesus loves, an amazing cycle is set in motion. First, our love for him grows. Our increasing love leads us to worship, which further deepens our relationship with him. Then, as we establish healthy, warmhearted relationships with others, our lives become a bridge to Jesus for those we love. In turn, our relationships with others become a support for us during times of discouragement and a delight during times of celebration. Do you see how love incites each God-ordained purpose and spurs us on to the next? Love is the essential ingredient!

I have to tell you about one more added bonus to the step of loving as Jesus loves. It is a cure for an affliction many of us have, which my friend calls *destination disease*. That great phrase describes being more concerned about getting to our destination than in finding delight on the journey. Learning to love causes us to linger in the company of others and find enjoyment and companionship along the way.

How do we begin growing in love? We start by understanding where we are. So, before we go any further, let's take a hard look inside our hearts and examine our capacity to love others. Do you ever catch yourself muttering, *People, get out of my way or I will run over you?* Perhaps you have thought, *I can get what I want if I put up with this person.* Or, maybe it is a good day for you when you feel that, even though many people are weird, most of them are worth the investment once you get to know them. If these feelings and thoughts sound like you, God may be wanting to give you a heart transplant!

TWO UNLIKELY CANDIDATES FOR LOVE

I know exactly how necessary a divine heart transplant can be, because I needed one myself. Loving others was definitely not easy for me, nor was it easy for my neighbor, Margie. I had a serious control-perfectionism problem about running my household; Margie used people at work to complete projects. Let me tell you about Margie first.

Margie was a weekly churchgoer and a corporate middle manager, but she didn't value people. Her modus operandi at work was, "Stay focused. Crank it out. Make it happen." She was an abrasive, task-oriented committee of one who did not have time for the slow-moving mechanism of relationships and collective wisdom. And her demanding boss always applauded her efforts: "You're a no-nonsense gal, a hard driver, an asset to our company." As long as Margie got things done and received affirmations like that, she didn't need to like people.

Then she got a new boss. After observing Margie and listening to complaints from her peers and subordinates for some time, he wrote her up for poor teamwork. His report substantially decreased her merit pay and annual bonus. Stunned, she began to question her management style. Her paradigm, "People are good for whatever you can get out of them," no longer worked. The cold, steel dominos of her self-righteousness started tumbling down, and she did not know what to do. How was she supposed to change?

Motivated by job security and money, Margie began considering some new options. She started with a simple prayer asking God to help her. Then she began thinking about what kind of person she needed to be to become a team player. As she did so, she realized that a team player is a person who has the ability to relish the adventure with others. She let that idea rattle around in her thinking but wasn't sure how to implement it. The concept didn't quite come together for her, and it seemed as if some facts were missing.

But God was at work. Next Margie heard a sermon about why we love—it is because Jesus first loved us.[2] Suddenly she understood the real reason she was called to love. Her life was to reflect Jesus' love for others and thereby draw them toward his love! Overwhelmed, she sobbed for several hours after church that day. She realized that she truly wanted to be a person who drew others to the adventure of a godly life.

With her newly discovered purpose of loving others and an immediate change of heart, Margie welcomed Jesus' gracious outpouring of love in a way she'd never known. From the overflow of that abundance, she tried something she had never done before. For the next several months, she focused on investing in the lives of people around her.

As Margie began to interact with people in a more loving manner, she was surprised that she truly liked a few of them. She even grew emotionally attached to several others. She began to care about her graphic designers, writers, and film crews as human beings with eternal souls. She began to look forward to interviewing applicants and welcoming new team members. For the first time in her life, Margie began to see projects as a way to develop friendships and support systems between people rather than seeing people as a way to complete projects!

During this complex step of her life, a curious thing happened to Margie. God began to use people in her life in such a powerful way that she now says she cannot live without the tender blessing of friendships. She now eagerly anticipates meeting one of her husband's new golf buddies or a woman at the gym. And when a coworker said, "Marg, God has never made a finer friend than you," she simply beamed!

To love is to receive a glimpse of heaven.
KAREN SUNDE,
PLAYWRIGHT

My challenge in the area of love was a bit different. I had camped out on this particular stepping-stone for years, so I knew God wanted me to love people. I wanted to love people too, but it wasn't easy when those people actually lived in my home (and I'm not talking about my children!). Let me explain.

I was a corporately downsized, single mother of two children whose father had died. I paid the mortgage by working from home for a start-up snowboard apparel company and by housing three international high school students. And that's where I had difficulty with love: I did not find it easy to love those students as Jesus loves me.

My hangup in this area is not too hard to understand. I am a classic, cautious introvert who needs more time than other personality types to nurture relationships outside my family and best-friend circle. I was also a perfectionist who considered my control issues to mean nothing more than that I was well schooled in the art of tough love. Plus, I was under enormous stress at the time, so I insisted on keeping a tidy house and expected people to give an attentive response to all my instructions. That scenario left little room for loving as Jesus loves.

I hate to admit it, but I managed my household in such a regimented manner that my self-imposed nickname was *Captain*, as in Captain von Trapp from *The Sound of Music*. The difference, however, was that my rules made von Trapp's look mild. I didn't have a whistle like von Trapp, but my voice was piercing, and I had no qualms about enforcing every rule.

Let me highlight some of those rules. Each household resident, including my two children, was assigned his or her own set of color-coordinated cups, dishes, and silverware labeled with his or her name.

This was the absolute rule: if you want to eat a family meal, make sure your dishes are washed.

Other equally tender rules followed:

- If you leave the toilet seat up, you will clean that toilet.
- If you don't do your laundry, you won't have clean underwear.
- If you don't make your lunch for school, you won't have a lunch to eat.
- If you don't put your shoes in the shoe cupboard, you won't find them anywhere when you need them.
- If you don't set your alarm for school, you'll be late with no note.

You may look at those rules and think, *Sign me up for your next parenting class!* But before you sign on the dotted line, take a closer look at my heart. Although my rules were certainly efficient, I desperately needed to tone down my caustic demeanor. I didn't understand the difference between lovingly setting up consequences for inappropriate behavior and abrasively controlling preteens and teens. Fortunately, God didn't allow me to remain in that place. He taught me a lesson about love by allowing me to be loved by the very ones to whom I had not expressed love.

> *I do not feel fulfilled putting toilet seats down all day.*
> Erma Bombeck

You see, I came down with a serious bout of pneumonia that left me bedridden for a week. While I was dependent on the kindness of my children and the three students with whom I shared my home, I finally figured out that I no longer wanted to be a hard-nosed disciplinarian. I wanted law and order, but not at the expense of love. God never intended for me to be unmercifully hard on others. He wanted me, through his love and grace, to help the kids mature, not to overpower them.

Make every effort to live in peace with all men and to be holy; without holiness no one will see the Lord. See to it that no one misses the grace of God and that no bitter root grows up to cause trouble and defile many. (HEBREWS 12:14–15)

Even though I had been aware of my problem and had prayed about solving it for years, I now shot petitions up to heaven about how I wanted to do life better. I wanted to live out Christlike love. My prayers began to be answered. I grabbed on to God's promise: "I will give you a new heart—I will give you new and right desires—and put a new spirit within you. I will take out your stony hearts of sin and give you new hearts of love."[3]

My gruffness at home started to wear off. My drill sergeant and boot-camp mentality began to soften and was replaced with love. As I left behind my unreachable Utopia and entered the real world of laughable flaws, I experienced a freedom I did not expect. Joining the ranks of imperfect people was a precious prize during this step in my life. I was still the type of woman who likes order in her home, but my transformation was a modern-day miracle for which I will be eternally grateful.

As God took me to a deeper level of understanding, it dawned on me that perhaps he had been waiting for me to step into my specific purpose of loving others as he had loved me. I realized that my student renters did not know Jesus and that I might be the only representative of Christ they ever got to know personally. It occurred to me that part of my purpose was to become an example of God's love to the people he was seeking to redeem. If that was true, my primary concern had to be: become the type of Christian they respected. I regret that I missed the mark with two of them before they moved out.

About that same time, God nudged me into a women's study and seated me next to the gracious Chaundel Holladay who, with her unconditional love for me, changed my life forever. When I first met her, I had no idea that God would use her to model my purpose in life: to love with the love of Jesus. Chaundel expressed interest in my well-being as an individual and as a Christian. She paid attention to me when I talked and she affirmed me. She invested in me and pursued me as a friend.

Because of the irreplaceable friendships I formed in that study with Chaundel, our group, and women in subsequent groups like it, I now better understand some sage advice of George Washington Carver. He once said to be tender with those who are young, compassionate with those who are old, and tolerant of those who are weak because at some point in life we will have been all of those.

> *The gift of love is an education in itself.*
> ELEANOR ROOSEVELT

If you were born a people person or an extrovert, it may be hard for you to understand why Margie and I struggled to open our hearts to love people. But please don't be smug about your God-given ability to easily relate to others. Instead, count your blessings that this step was easier for you than some of the others will be. And, regardless of where we are when we take this step, our love for others can always mature to become more like the love of Jesus.

THE SOJOURNER'S GUIDE TO LOVING OTHERS

If your desire is to grow in the love of Jesus and express that love through your relationships with others, then you're ready to have God reveal more about your life purposes. Take time out to consider and follow through on the suggestions below. They will help you develop your relationships and nurture your love.

Catch Yourself Making a Loving Difference

For one week, make a note of anything you do that makes a loving difference in someone's life. This exercise will raise your awareness that you are fulfilling one of your life purposes by endeavoring to love God's people. It will be an affirmation for you. If you can't catch yourself making a loving difference, don't hire a detective to follow you around in case you missed something! Start looking for daily opportunities to love others.

Get Connected at Church

If you haven't done so already, become involved in a local church. Participate in a small group for fellowship and Bible study. The depth and longevity of church family friendships may surprise you and bless you for many years to come.

Offer Forgiveness

Forgive someone today. Don't put it off. Stop analyzing the pros and cons. Simply pray for the right timing and do it. Forgive in honor of Jesus' forgiveness of you. If you need to forgive yourself, the advice is the same: just do it!

Take a Relational Opportunities Checkup

What opportunities do you have at this time to develop specific relational habits such as those listed here?

- If you have lost a job, have you considered joining a business networking group?
- If your spouse died some time ago, is now the time to begin building new relationships through outings, socializing, or dating?
- If you have you been working on building a strong marriage, have you been bonding and communicating with your husband by going on regularly scheduled dates?
- If you have had a miscarriage, have you considered letting others in a similar situation help you by joining a support group?
- If you have been attempting to kick an addiction—whether it be to cigarettes, gambling, pornography, sex, alcohol, drugs, or

food—have you begun your recovery with the help of a support group or clinic?

🍃 If you need guidance regarding your finances, faith, family, or vocation, have you sought out a Christian counselor or mentor who can advise you?

🍃 If you are trying to discern your purposes in life, have you read *Conversations on Purpose for Women* in this series and chosen a Purpose Partner (a coach) to process information in a conversational format?

No matter what you determine your relational needs to be at this time, ask God to fill the needs first and foremost with himself. Then, ask him if it would be beneficial for you to invite someone to walk alongside you. Your church may have a variety of systems in place to help you with relationships, or you may want to start a group tailored to your needs.[4] You could also concentrate on meeting new people or nurturing an existing friendship. Just remember, though, that both established and new friendships require you to invest yourself in others.

Tell God that you are willing to open your heart wide, to risk fear and vulnerability, in order to grow in love. He knows that loving relationships are packed with tears and laughter, and that they can stimulate new attitudes and action. Ask him to take you from where you are today to where he wants you to be.

Pray for the Unloving and Unlovable

Relationships are not always pretty. Some are unbelievably ugly. One of the great sacrifices of love is to pray for those who are unlovely and unloving . . . even those who have harmed us. I encourage you to ask God to help you learn to do this. Remember that warm feelings and emotional enjoyment are not the goals of love. Love is caring about God's eternal relationship with others. Pray for God's best in the lives of those you find troublesome or difficult. Ask God to shape your perspective with his.

Some of us have had to learn hard lessons about boundaries, trust, commitment, hatred, bigotry, codependency, abuse, or neglect. If this has been your experience, you should not take lightly the emotional, physical, and spiritual dangers of these problems. I urge you to get immediate, professional help for any lingering, detrimental effects.

RECOMMENDED BOOKS ON LOVING OTHERS

Boundaries, by Henry Cloud and John Townsend[5]
As Iron Sharpens Iron, by Howard and William Hendricks[6]

NOW IS THE TIME TO LOVE OTHERS

Will you take this next step toward God and his purpose for your life: *to love each other as Jesus loves you*? Have you opened your heart to loving Jesus more by loving all types of people? Are you looking for new opportunities to love each day?

The Bible says, "If I speak in the tongues of men and of angels, but have not love, I am only a resounding gong or a clanging cymbal."[7] That verse uses strong language to communicate God's will for your life. Do you want to be an on-purpose woman of healthy relationships? Then commit to a decisive action step today.

May God wrap his loving arms around you as you walk through this important relational time and discern more about your life purposes. May you be filled with every good blessing because of our Lord's extreme love for you. May you be acutely aware of the value of this step—to love others as Jesus loves—all the way into eternity.

GOD'S WISDOM FOR THE PATHWAY

THE "RUTH" STEP OF LIFE: LOVE EACH OTHER AS JESUS LOVES YOU

For a lesson from Ruth, a loving daughter-in-law to Naomi, read Ruth 1–4. Ruth teaches us about love, loyalty, kindness, and faithfulness. How strong is your love for your family and extended family? For *all* of them? Pray that God will reveal to you one particular relationship in which he would like you to invest more love, time, energy, and/or resources.

Personal Pathway Questions

1. How successful have you been lately in obeying God's command to "love one another"?

2. With whom do you currently have a healthy relationship? This list of groups may help you think of specific names:
   - Church
   - Christian ministry friends
   - Clubs/organizations
   - Community volunteers
   - Extended family
   - Gym
   - Immediate family
   - Neighbors
   - Parents of children's friends
   - Small group
   - School
   - Sports
   - Support group
   - Work

3. With whom do you currently have an unhealthy relationship? (Hint: Just think of those whose company encourages you to avoid God or stimulates sinful thoughts or actions.)

4. Healthy relationships are a prayerful choice. Is cultivating or terminating a particular relationship more critical to your spiritual well-being right now? What is God nudging you to do about one or more of your relationships?

NOTES

1. (p. 64) John 15:9a, 12–13.
2. (p. 67) See 1 John 4:19.
3. (p. 70) Ezekiel 36:26, TLB.
4. (p. 73) Visit the Saddleback Church website at www.saddleback.com for a sample of church-based relational programs, such as Celebrate Recovery, LifeMates, Woman to Woman Mentoring, support groups, and C.L.A.S.S. 101 called "Introduction to Our Church Family."
5. (p. 74) Henry Cloud and John Townsend, *Boundaries* (Grand Rapids: Zondervan, 1992).
6. (p. 74) Howard and William Hendricks, *As Iron Sharpens Iron* (Chicago: Moody Press, 1995).
7. (p. 74) 1 Corinthians 13:1.

Part Three

Follow *in* Jesus' Footsteps

God's *Discipleship* Purpose for You:
To Know Christ and Become Like Him

Chapter 5

PURSUE PEACE

Seek peace and pursue it.
(PSALM 34:14)

Stop for a moment and take a look back at your progress along the
pathway to purpose. You have at least begun the difficult step of *for-*
getting what is behind and pressing on toward the goal, so you are traveling lighter, no longer weighed down by all the burdens of your past.
You have realized that your most obvious purpose is right before your
eyes—on today's to-do list. You now know that *doing what matters*
today is not just a tedious obstacle but, in fact, the means by which
God is preparing you for and leading you toward his grand, unique
purpose for you. You have also discovered that the challenge of *loving*
others as Jesus loves you is the essential ingredient that ignites every other
God-ordained purpose in your life. I hope you now can begin to see
the great strides you are making toward God's call on your life. So far,
so good!

Our next stepping-stone, *seek peace and pursue it*, may well be the
most sought-after rock in the entire stream. Peace can be described as
a state of mind that is free from annoyance, distraction, and anxiety. It
is a quiet knowing that God can be trusted. It provides undeniable
serenity and calm within your soul that is worth far more than gold.

Women want peace, and they want it badly. Peace is as much in demand as a brand-name, classic pump at a shoe sale!

There's only one problem, and that would be the *pursuit* part. It has been rumored that this highly prized stone is slightly submerged underwater, so you may sink ankle-deep before you are able to locate it and stand firmly upon it. But please, take my advice and be true to your heart's longing for peace. Don't hesitate for a second to plunge your foot into the stream. Inner peace not only sounds appealing, it is worth the cost of the pursuit, particularly if you have been feeling distracted, unhappy, or dissatisfied with life.

I must have been asleep in church as a kid because I never gave the Psalm 34:14 idea, *seek peace and pursue it*, much thought. I definitely didn't think of that sweet-sounding passage as a command from God. But the verse is written in the imperative voice. Remember that lesson from your high school English class? An imperative means that we should read it as if the word *you* were in front of each verb. Doing so results in a strong statement: *you* seek peace, and *you* pursue it.

Imagine the implications of fulfilling this imperative. You are to seek peace day in and day out, whether it is easy or difficult. You are to pursue peace when you don't feel well, when someone hurts your feelings, or even when a loved one dies. You are to seek peace. Amen.

WHAT MAKES PEACE SO PRECIOUS?

First and foremost, peace is precious because of where we find it. I frantically searched the world for peace, but ended up confused. I have since learned that finding peace has far more to do with sitting in Jesus' presence, listening to him, than in doing anything else. And what a blessing that is!

As we grow in intimacy with Jesus, we learn to recognize God's voice, which makes it easier for us to understand our current and long-term assignments from him. We are able to more easily accept his perspective and expert advice about the important issues of life such as family matters, financial decisions, and commitments that could otherwise distract us from his purposes. Who but our Lord would give us a specific purpose to pursue peace and then arrange it so that our pursuit would lead us to hearing his will in all areas of life? What a stress reliever!

Peace is also precious because obeying God's command to seek and pursue peace gives you a bona fide focus for today. I wish I had known that learning how to be peaceful was a worthy purpose in and of itself. I would have been spared years of tears had I known that peace was a stepping-stone that would lead me toward God and his other purposes for my life. I didn't realize that craving peace was normal, so I struggled to understand my hunger for peace as if I had a dreaded disease. Had I known that finding peace was my God-intended goal, I would have felt on track instead of out of kilter much of the time.

INNER PEACE FIASCO: PARTY OF THREE

No matter how important the stepping-stone of seeking peace is on the pathway to purpose, no matter how much we want it, and no matter how simple God has made the pursuit of it, some of us will still have difficulty finding it. I certainly did, and I know I'm not alone. At one point, two friends and I were so frustrated by our search for peace that we began meeting together to explore our current understanding and to encourage one another on our journey. As we shared our stories with each other, we enjoyed some good laughs because we truly had been a peace-seeking fiasco in triplicate!

Danielle, a friend from college days, complained of feeling restless and agitated. Overspending and busyness were her pain relievers. Like many of her friends in her urban, concrete jungle, she was becoming disillusioned by the greedy and gluttonous attitude of her frenetic life. It screamed, "More! Faster! Bigger! Better!" She felt like a fashionable gerbil on a Gucci treadmill. She ran—but to what end?

At age thirty-five, she was miserable. Her lack of peace was slowly destroying her. She had grown weary of creating expensive diversions—

such as her recent helicopter ride to a local island for a weekend get-away—just to fight the vague feeling of being a failure in the important things of life. She realized that whatever contentment she was looking for could not be generated by a financial vortex, fast cars, or fast men. What was the cure?

Across town from Danielle lived Becky. For years, Becky believed that her catalyst for inner peace would be to identify her most unique life purpose. If only she could figure out the main task God wanted her to accomplish before she died, she would find peace. But by age forty-two, all of her attempts to conjure up a spectacular gift for God had left her discontented. She had never been able to sustain a ministry after the razzle-dazzle of the start-up. She had no idea why everything fizzled out. She felt cheated out of her chance to leave a legacy.

Becky's frustration was becoming intolerable. Despite her strong religious upbringing and all the appearances of a good life, she felt as if she were living life in her sleep, drowning in apathy, fatigued beyond tears. She was even convinced that she must have a serious medical problem. So Becky made a decision. She would abandon her fruitless search for an elaborate meaning for her life. She would give up trying to find the "one thing" that would provide a sense of sacred ambition and fulfillment. Instead, she would turn her limited energy toward learning to be content in spite of the disappointment and deep personal void she felt. Her only question was, "How do I do this?"

> *Inner peace is the road to world peace.*[1]
> MAIREAD CORRIGAN MAGUIRE, NOBEL PEACE LAUREATE

At about the time Danielle, Becky, and I began to meet together, I had traveled perhaps an inch farther down the road toward peace than they had, so they asked me to be the fearless leader of our small group! "Ladies," I said late one evening, "I think it's time I told you more specifics about my unfinished journey. I have been a Christian for most of my life, yet for years I had been unable to determine why I had no peace. My constant state of being perturbed had become an ugly sight to me. I had grown tired of the sour, scowling image I saw reflected in my mirror. In desperation, I launched a full-scale, no-holds-barred search for serenity. It was a watershed choice for me. I did not give myself the option of turning back."

Danielle and Becky wanted to hear all the gory details of my great escape before we wrapped up for the evening. I didn't have the heart to tell them that I had found answers but I still didn't know what to do with them. Although I had not yet taken a safe stance on this stepping-stone, I began to tell my story.

I SIMPLY *MUST* FIND PEACE!

Approximately one year after my apparently unfruitful trip to India, I decided to schedule a personal, spiritual retreat somewhere— anywhere—in the world. I viewed this as my last-ditch effort to loosen the stranglehold that purposelessness and lack of peace had on me. I figured that once I experienced the quiet life, I would begin to feel better. There simply had to be a proven method for purposeless people to become serene and peaceful. I was not willing to wade through any textbooks on serenity, so a retreat, sprinkled with a few lectures from some peaceful folks, sounded like what I wanted.

Soon after that decision, I was in the library doing some graduate research on women in leadership. My heart started pounding loudly as I read about the seven women who had been awarded the Nobel Peace Prize. Only three of those women were still alive.[2] To my delight, one was Mother Teresa, and I had already met her. The other two were Mairead Corrigan Maguire and Betty Williams Smith, who had teamed up to try to stop the war in Northern Ireland.

I sat in the library, mesmerized. Certainly I would find clarity on peace if I met all of the living women Nobel Peace laureates! It didn't matter to me that the lessons from Mother Teresa hadn't yet jelled in my mind. I instinctively knew that I had to meet the other two women, or at least their coworkers, who would be able to tell me all about their leaders. I had to follow this trail! I had no idea that God was coaxing me along. I never suspected that he was using the perfect bait—my passion for travel—to lead me toward an understanding of how purpose, prayer, and peacefulness are linked.

Before fear had a chance to set in, I dialed the office of the Peace People in Northern Ireland, a group Mairead had cofounded to promote nonviolence. A cheerful-sounding woman with a heavy Irish accent answered, "This is Mairead Maguire."

I couldn't believe it! Was I actually speaking to her? Grasping the phone tightly in my shaking hand, I gave voice to my doubts right into her Nobel laureate ear: "Who—who is this?" I must have sounded like an owl. As I fumbled through the conversation, Mairead invited me to the Benburb Monastery in Northern Ireland for the Peace People's annual conference. She would be there for the conference although Betty Williams Smith would not be able to attend. I accepted and quickly negotiated an invitation for my mom to go with me.

As we conversed about the arrangements, Mairead suggested, "Why don't you and your mum participate in our three-day fast for peace during the conference?" I promised her that we'd think about it. But the truth is, I lied to buy myself time until I could invent an excuse to get out of it gracefully. After all, I didn't want to wreck my vacation with a fast that had nothing to do with me. The last time I had fasted had *not* been for world peace; it had been to get into a little black dress.

When I asked my mom if she'd like to go to Belfast with me, she answered, "No thanks. I don't want to go. It's too dangerous."

I was shocked! How could my traveling buddy bail on me? "You're going! You owe me for taking you to Calcutta," I countered. "I got you an engraved invitation from a Nobel laureate. It'll be fun! Come on!"

We continued our specialized version of arguing for a while, but I finally won. "I neeeeed you to go with me," I whined. What mother could resist that pull on her heartstrings from a daughter who had been sad for so long? She agreed to go.

After my two kids gave me their final hugs and reminded me to bring them lots of cool stuff, they headed out on a summer vacation extravaganza of their own. My mom and I once again donned our backpacks and headed to the airport. My dad was our chauffeur, fulfilling what he jokingly referred to as his life calling—to drop us off at the airport and then stay close to home as our prayer warrior!

This time I was convinced I would find the answers about peace and life purpose that I so desperately wanted. I still had no idea that my overseas searches were the handiwork of God nor did I suspect that purpose and peace were interwoven threads in his tapestry of my life.

For several days after our arrival in Northern Ireland, my mom and I drank in the lush, green countryside. We giggled through our first-ever bed-and-breakfast experience, which Mairead so graciously had arranged for us. Then the big day arrived. It was time to go live in an old monastery; sleep on hard, narrow beds; and meet with *holy people* about how to live in peace with one another. My mom grimaced at me and said, "Remind me again why I let you talk me into this!"

We hadn't been at the conference for more than an hour before we realized that the attendees were on their thirty-seventh day of a forty-day, liquid-only fast for peace. (Some of the "less holy" ones had eaten bread on Wednesdays and Fridays!) I was stunned by the contradiction between my way of life and the Peace People's self-denial. Stunned, yes. Convicted to join the fast, no.

While in Northern Ireland, I caught glimpses of why they were committed to such a sacrificial fast. They were imploring God for peace in their beloved country. Within the span of just a few days, I had witnessed armored cars and militia with machine guns cruising the streets. I had wandered innocently into the middle of a city park standoff between the colorfully kilted representatives of the Protestant Orange and the Catholic Green. At first, I thought it was a

> *Those who are peacemakers will plant seeds of peace and reap a harvest of goodness.*
> (JAMES 3:18, TLB)

parade. When reality hit, I got myself out of that park as quickly as my legs could carry me.

During my visit, the stakes in my personal search for peace were raised substantially. God connected the dots for me between my near-danger encounter, the images of my visit so far, and the words of Mairead, "Inner peace is the road to world peace." Her words penetrated my heart, and in a flash I saw what I had never seen before. My search wasn't only about me. My quest and its outcome mattered in the larger scope of things. I saw that each of us needs to be part of the world's solution, not part of the problem. Finally I understood the global *why*, but I still lacked the personal *how*.

One evening Mairead invited me for a chat that she allowed me to audiotape. We kicked off our shoes and sat on her bed in the dormitory. She said, "Kate, you traveled across the ocean to find a well-known woman leader in order to ask how to develop inner peacefulness and serenity. You thought that because I've been fortunate enough to talk with the Pope and Mother Teresa, presidents and queens, surely I would have the answer and be able to help you on your mission.

"But now you're shocked to find a regular lady who believes that the key to inner and world peace is the sharing of ourselves and our possessions with others less fortunate. You're surprised to see that I'm the same as other people: I mend, I cook, I clean, I have dishes in the sink, I volunteer for the Peace People, I try to be a good wife to my husband Jackie, I do some yoga, I pray all through the day, and I scold my five children in between peace conferences.

"Two answers about finding inner peace seem quite clear to me in your case. First of all, be a good mother to your children. Second, listen to God, perhaps several hours a day, as you go about your work. You'll soon be able to hear him, and not so much your own voice."

Those are not the sophisticated answers I've been hoping for, I thought to myself. I had spent thousands of dollars traveling thousands of miles to get some action items for my "Serenity To-Do List." So much for that investment!

I was looking for a quick fix. I had anticipated that Mairead would tell me that Nobel Peace laureates find tranquility by taking long vacations every couple of months to do pious contemplation. I thought she would say that peace can be found by getting subscriptions to religious book clubs, by playing only Christian music on our radios, or by throwing out our television sets to keep our minds pure. I wanted something to do or accomplish, never realizing that *doing* was the opposite of *being*!

Mairead saw that I was having a hard time with the simplicity of her advice. So the next day she called me aside and sweetly counseled me to relax, rest my brain, enjoy life, smile, be a good person, and treat others with the deepest respect. She said, "Pray and listen closely to God all day long. Be faithful to him. Tell God you're a vehicle for him. If he wants you to do something, he'll let you know. He may want you to do dishes at a mission house; it is simply your job to listen for instructions. Be kind and warm to people, especially your family and those closest to you, and you will find peace." Then, she inscribed a book for me: "Pray, pray, pray, all day long!"

> *Pray without ceasing.*
> (1 THESSALONIANS 5:17, NASB)

So my mom and I headed home. In light of Mairead's graciousness to us, I immediately began to feel bad about several things. One was that my mom and I had gone to great lengths to make it appear that we had been fasting. The others did not know that we had secret candy bar stashes in our backpacks. They did not know that when those ran out we raided the monastery kitchen in the middle of the night. Like little hamsters, we had stuffed our cheeks with boiled cabbage and potatoes. I had gone to Northern Ireland to become holy, but I had come home a liar and a thief.

I was no more peaceful upon my return home than when I began my trip. Mairead's counsel, that prayerfulness brings peacefulness, had not yet sunk in. I began to feel guilty that a second Nobel Peace laureate had eloquently stated what I needed to hear, but I wasn't spiritually mature enough to comprehend it or act on it. I wasn't quite ready to *get it*.

SEARCHING FOR PEACE: ROUND TWO

I was concerned that Danielle and Becky would be frustrated with my inability to have the answers all of us wanted. I hoped that telling them the details of my pursuit of peace would at least give us something about which to think and talk. It did. The next time we met, we jumped into dialogue before we even sat down.

Becky said, "So, I've been thinking a lot about your story, and it seems to me—from what you've said—that prayerfulness invites peacefulness, which in turn, probably enables us to hear God when he shares more about our unique life purpose! So, in a real sense, all we have to do while we wait for a grand life purpose is to do nothing—except pray and listen for God's voice."

Danielle added, "It is just like the verse that says, 'Be still, and know that I am God.'"[3]

"I think that's the key," I answered. Then I summarized for them what I more recently had heard others say on the topic. I explained that God can give a purpose to anyone he chooses at any time, whether she is peaceful or not, but that listening to him is an enormous gift we give to ourselves. I told them that we grow and learn as we spend time with him because we become more attuned to his ways and his character. In turn, we begin to fall more in love with him, which causes us to want to be obedient to his will. Then, when we least expect it, we find that we have become more receptive to impressions from him regarding our life purpose. As we begin to understand our next immediate step, we don't feel as driven to have all the long-range answers. Step by step our faith increases, and we learn to trust that God does have a plan for our lives.

"I think that's the way it works," I said. Then I added that I thought it best to balance the "do nothing" extreme with the perspective of the

Inner Peace Checklist (below). I explained that I realized I was making some progress when I could answer yes to some of the questions on the list.

INNER PEACE CHECKLIST

As you pursue peace in your life, are you:

- Enjoying the company of God while you're doing chores such as laundry or dishes?

- Craving longer, more frequent, private appointments with the Holy Spirit?

- Finding peace about upcoming, difficult decisions by reading and meditating on biblical truths?

- Seeing the value of recording in a spiritual journal your spiritual milestones, conversations with God, and questions for him?

- Recognizing that God is working on your behalf, even during your moments of anxiety and disquiet?

- Getting a good laugh out of the song, "I Did It My Way"?

- Teaching your children or others to listen to God—and being humbled by the life-changing results?

FINDING PEACE, DAY BY DAY

When I stopped meeting with Danielle and Becky years ago, I did not yet feel that I had the peace I wanted. In fact, I never would have guessed that it was already on its way. Unbeknown to me, God had been growing the seeds that Mairead had so tenderly planted in my heart about serenity. He was drawing me closer to him. He was calling additional people into my life who diligently watered those ideas with their words and role modeling.

For example, during many of the years I had searched for inner peace, I often listened intently to a young pastor named Jeff Walling. He encouraged me to establish regularly scheduled quiet times of Bible reading. He said to start with three-minute sessions and see where God would lead. As I practiced that spiritual discipline, I could feel myself being drawn into the arms of Jesus. I discovered that nothing compared to those few minutes a day with Jesus, the miracle worker.

Much later, as I spent longer periods of time reading Scripture, one insight led to another. I came to realize, for example, that the control issues of depression, fear, and perfectionism run in packs, all feeding off the same decaying carcass of hopelessness. Once I became aware of that deadly triune of "peace busters," I asked God to turn my powerlessness against those things into strength and boldness. Over the course of several years, God was gracious enough to do that for me.

> *I planted the seed, Apollos watered it, but God made it grow.*
> (1 CORINTHIANS 3:6)

Eventually, I began to experience God speaking in the silence of my soul. One day during my quiet time I caught a glimpse of how far God had brought me toward peace. In amazement I wrote in my journal, "Thank you, Jesus, for showing me how to find peace. You modeled it by going off alone to pray and listen to your Father. I want to learn to listen to God, my Father, throughout the entire day." What a phenomenal privilege it is to hear God speak. I am so grateful for the inner peace he has granted me and look forward to growing more peaceful every day.

So, what about you? Where would you place yourself on the Inner Peace Richter Scale?

Full-Fledged Frantic	Semi-Serene	At Peace
Annoyed, distracted, and anxious	Having some calm within your soul	Having an undeniable security

No matter what your starting point, the fundamental question about finding peace is the same: Is your heart hungry enough to *pursue* peace? Will you take the time to be still in God's presence and take in whatever he offers you? God is waiting for you to take this step so that he can open your eyes to all that he has in store for you.

THE SOJOURNER'S GUIDE TO PURSUING PEACE

The following suggestions will help you in your pursuit of inner peace. Take as much time as needed to put each of these into practice. As always, resist the temptation to cut corners!

Practice Silence

Create opportunities for God to speak to you by practicing silence. Do your part by reducing noise, stimuli, and information overload. Turn off your television, stereo, and car radio. Gracefully bow out of a loud, multi-voiced conversation. Spend time in a library or museum. Ask God daily to make you a better listener. Ask him to take you from where you are today to where he always intended you to be.

For a more focused time of silence, sit on a patio swing with a glass of iced tea and the Holy Spirit, but without a stack of paperwork to read—and without worrying that you'll be tried and convicted as a goof-off. Words of caution: be prepared to have people wonder what you're doing. Be willing to say, "Nothing!" The more you practice quietness in your life, the more opportunities you will find to be silent before the Lord.

Stop the Endless Mind Chatter

The path to peace is paved with long stretches of silence. Often, the most damaging noise comes from internal mind chatter. Do you constantly talk to yourself (silently or out loud)? If so, it is time to stop the brain noise. Stop torturing yourself. You don't have to be your own captive audience. Tell yourself to be quiet.

Shoot Bullet Prayers to Heaven All Day Long

Train yourself in the habit of talking to and listening to God all day, every day. This week, try shooting off speeding-bullet prayers regarding everything you do. Then, slow down to enjoy God's replies. Expect answers on all aspects of your character development, roles, relationships, finances, purposes, and more.

Don't Feel Guilty about Silence That Puts You to Sleep or Makes You Nap!

If you are physically tired or emotionally exhausted, you may fall asleep while you're trying to listen to God. Not to worry. Resting is biblical. God even rested on the seventh day! On some days it seems like I can pray forever, but on other days I nod off as soon as I sit down to pray.

Remember that rest nurtures the body, soul, and mind. A nap during your prayer time can be an excellent, no-cost therapy for whatever is ailing you. I don't consider naps a luxury; they have always been necessary for my sanity. So nap if you need to. I just did! And I'm in good company. Churchill, Einstein, and presidents Kennedy and Reagan took naps too! So nap because you can! Don't feel guilty about it, just continue praying when you wake up.

Purposely Change Your Pace

Learn to slow down. One helpful thing you can do as you pursue peace is to make a conscientious effort to eliminate the pressure of *performing* for a while. Instead of performing at record speeds, do just the opposite. Consider a hobby such as painting, reading, or fishing that may quiet your soul. Adapting daily, weekly, monthly, and annual habits that purposefully change the pace of life may be one of the most difficult suggestions to implement in this entire book for a busy or driven person. Slowing down, however, greatly increases peacefulness.

If you absolutely can't lessen your pace right now because of crises, deadlines, or commitments, take frequent, brief time-outs. Look for creative ways to slow down. Feel free to try my top ten favorite ways to change my pace when I'm under too much pressure: take a walk, pray, recall a Scripture verse, sing a song out loud, dance to the music from *Zorba the Greek*, window shop for a few minutes while running errands, write a letter of encouragement, ride a bike around the block, swim a few laps, or just sit in the car and laugh while it goes through the car wash!

Avoid Peace Killers

Adjust your priorities to stay away from three surefire peace killers: people-pleasing, keeping up with the Joneses, and worrying about things that are out of your control. The next time you catch yourself in one of these traps, talk to a friend about holding you accountable to stop it.

RECOMMENDED BOOKS ON INNER PEACE

The Overload Syndrome, by Dr. Richard Swenson[4]
Ordering Your Private World, by Gordon McDonald[5]
Surviving Information Overload, by Kevin Miller[6]

NOW IS THE TIME TO FIND INNER PEACE

Will you take this next step toward God and his purpose for your life by *seeking peace and pursuing it*? Will you listen to God throughout the entire day? The Bible tells us:

Don't worry about anything; instead, pray about everything. Tell God what you need, and thank him for all he has done. If you do this, you will experience God's peace, which is far more wonderful than the human mind can understand. His peace will guard your hearts and minds as you live in Christ Jesus.[7]

Are you ready to be God's woman of inner peace? Then I encourage you to put prayer first in your life. Doing so will help you find a peace that makes it easier to hear God speak to you. Listen closely as he reveals more about himself and your unique purpose in his plans. My heart's desire for you is that you will make the commitment to pursue peace. It will make a world of difference. It will change your life forever!

GOD'S WISDOM FOR THE PATHWAY

THE "MARTHA VS. MARY" STEP OF LIFE: PURSUE PEACE

For a lesson from two sisters, Martha and Mary, read Luke 10:38–42. For many of us, this is a difficult story to hear, because we have so many responsibilities to juggle. On any given day, we are much more like Martha, busy serving others, and we forget that Jesus wants to spend time with us. Has busyness prevented you from being with the Lord? If so, how about starting today to seek his companionship and peace *in the midst of it all*?

Too often we are made to feel that "it's Mary's way or no way." The truth is that, in addition to sitting—uninterrupted—at our Lord's feet daily (like Mary), we also need to ask Jesus to join us in all the hectic moments of our lives (which Martha was too frazzled to do). Just imagine Jesus hoping to be invited into Martha's kitchen for a long chat as they worked together.

Personal Pathway Questions

1. How well do you listen to God throughout the entire day?

2. Write anything you currently do that encourages you to pursue peace by listening to God. Consider the following list:

   - Attitude of constant listening
   - Bible study time
   - Bullet prayers
   - Creating silence
   - Journaling
   - Prayer
   - Quiet time (reflection)
   - Reducing busyness
   - Spiritual fasting
   - Private or community worship (singing or instrumental music)

3. Which of the ideas from Question 2 would you like to experiment with to increase your desire to listen?

4. What makes it difficult for you to hear God? What can you do to lessen the difficulty?

5. Did you realize before reading this chapter that pursuing peace is a God-intended purpose for your life? Or, that you can pursue peace by praying and listening to God? What does this information teach a woman who says, "I just want to know my life purpose"?

6. What is God nudging you to do about pursuing peace?

NOTES

1. (p. 82) Conversations with the author at Benburb Monastery, Northern Ireland, during the Peace People's conference, 5–8 August , 1988. Used with permission. Mairead is the author of *The Vision of Peace: Faith and Hope in Northern Ireland* (New York: Orbis, 1999).

2. (p. 83) There were seven recipients at the time. As of 2004, twelve women have received the Nobel Peace Prize: Baroness Bertha von Suttner, Jane Addams, Emily Green Balch, Betty Williams and Mairead Corrigan, Mother Teresa, Alva Myrdal, Aung San Suu Kyi, Rigoberta Menchú Tum, Jody Williams, Shirin Ebadi, and Wangari Maathai.

3. (p. 88) Psalm 46:10.

4. (p. 93) Richard A. Swenson, *The Overload Syndrome* (Colorado Springs: NavPress, 1998).

5. (p. 93) Gordon McDonald, *Ordering Your Private World*, revised ed. (Nashville: Thomas Nelson, 2003).

6. (p. 93) Kevin Miller, *Surviving Information Overload* (Grand Rapids: Zondervan, 2004).

7. (p. 93) Philippians 4:6–7, NLT.

Chapter 6

REPENT OF ALL YOUR OFFENSES

"Repent! Turn away from all your offenses;
then sin will not be your downfall.
Rid yourselves of all the offenses you have committed,
and get a new heart and a new spirit."
(EZEKIEL 18:30–31)

Before you attempt this next step, I want you to lift your head, stretch, take a deep breath, and look around. Ahead of you, sunlight dances across the far bank, making it even more enticing than when you started. And behind you . . . well, did you have any idea how far you have come? I want you to have that encouragement in mind before you attempt the next step because it is one of the most difficult.

The stepping-stone, *repent and turn away from all your offenses*, causes many women to do a hesitation step, almost as if they are taking salsa lessons. (Step forward, left foot. Rock back, right foot.) Just imagine that sight for a minute. From afar, you notice a woman carefully navigating a stream, when suddenly she appears to be dodging a swarm of bees. She rocks back and forth in confusion, no dance-floor grace whatsoever. You can tell she's losing her balance, but there's nothing you can do to help her. Her only hope is to regroup and calmly and carefully proceed to the next well-worn stone.

What is it about repentance that makes us hesitate? I think we all know the answer. Repentance requires that we honestly appraise our sin life and adjust our thoughts and deeds accordingly. That's never easy. It requires trusting God with our frailties and failures, persevering against temptation, practicing a prayerful lifestyle, and being willing to make deeply personal changes.

Although this step is intimidating, please take it. I'll even walk with you as you step forward. I've logged many salsa steps in this vicinity of the stream, so I know it well. I've hesitated, fallen into the water, even scraped my knees on the way down, and I have the scars to prove it! Despite the injuries, I must tell you that each faltering attempt has been worth it.

When we repent and move away from sin, God is pleased. When we repent, we are better able to hear him and focus on the purposes for which we were born. In fact (and I didn't know this years ago), God may intentionally keep our life purpose out of focus because of our sin.

It took me a long time to learn that my character formation (less sinning, more repenting, and greater obedience) was far more important to God than anything I could ever hope to accomplish for him. If I had known that bit of information, which paints a more complete picture of God's intimate plan for us, I think I would have been busily occupied with my spiritual growth for years. I may even have been semicontent with my efforts while I waited to hear more from him.

WHY IS SIN SUCH A BIG DEAL?

In God's eyes, sin is really serious business. So before we go any farther, let's take a closer look at sin and its consequences. Sin is a deliberate turning away from God, a violation against him that separates us from him.

Just so there's no confusion about what sin is, the Bible lists many examples. Here are a few mentioned in the book of Ephesians: sensuality that indulges in every kind of impurity, lust, deceitful desires, falsehood, anger, stealing, unwholesome talk, bitterness, rage, brawling, slander, every form of malice, greed, obscenity, foolish talk, coarse joking, idolatry, deeds of darkness, drunkenness, and debauchery.[1] And that's just a partial list from one book!

> *"Go now and leave your life of sin."*
> (JOHN 8:11)

Repentance is remorse or sincere contrition for our sinful conduct. It is regret and sorrow that lead to a willingness to change. Did you catch the word *change*? *Change* makes all the difference. You see, sin can prompt two kinds of sorrow. *Human* sorrow, which in relationship to sin, is often nothing more than frustration and wounded pride that we got caught. *Godly* sorrow, on the other hand, is produced by the Holy Spirit in accordance with the will of God. Godly sorrow desires to keep the rich closeness of our relationship with God. It is a longing to do whatever is necessary to be holy before him.

When we truly repent, our words of contrition will match our subsequent actions. The new person we become gives evidence of our repentance. This critical truth is emphasized in Acts 26:20, where Paul says, "I preached that they should repent and turn to God and prove their repentance by their deeds."

Do you now see why repentance and purpose must go hand in hand? After we confess (or admit) our sin to God and turn away from it, our changed life turns us toward God. As we draw closer to God, we are better able to hear from him about our life's purpose; as we discern our life's purpose, we draw closer to God. In contrast, sin will always push us away from God, away from his voice, and away from his purposes.

STUMBLING OVER SIN

Sin is a universal problem that interferes with the healthy personal growth of every person. It especially interferes with our desire to fulfill God's purposes in life. I would guess that you identify with at least some of these pervasive sins: selfishness, jealousy, self-doubt, stubbornness, greed, laziness, judgmental attitude, rage, addictions/obsessions, and instant gratification. (If you can't identify with any of these, just wait thirty seconds while God triggers your memory and brings an example to mind!)

This list of troublesome sins didn't come from the Bible, although it could have. It didn't come from Harvard's latest national study on mentally unhealthy women. It came from my interviews with teenage boys who were incarcerated in a maximum-security facility for murder, rape, and/or burglary. (I should explain that I had asked to interview female inmates for a research project, "Roadblocks to God's Plan in a Young Person's Life," and somehow ended up in a boys' jail. The gender didn't really matter—at least I was in!)

In private sessions with the inmates, monitored by a guard outside the door, I asked each young man to name the three biggest stumbling blocks he would face if he were miraculously released from jail that day. I explained that he was not to include problems that pointed blame at family, friends, or a lack of employment or money. (I wanted the boys to concentrate on their personal characteristics and habits rather than play the "I'm a victim" game.) Those hard-core kids knew exactly what personal weaknesses would destroy their hopes for a decent life. They listed all the stumbling blocks (aka sins) you just read.

My next question was, "What three suggestions do you have for getting past those stumbling blocks?" Rephrased in more socially acceptable vocabulary, their responses are listed in the "Principles for Living a Better Life."

PRINCIPLES FOR LIVING A BETTER LIFE: ADVICE FROM YOUNG INMATES

1. Take one day at a time. Don't get ahead of yourself.

2. Identify distractions early, so you can eliminate them.

3. Think positively. Avoid negative people and influences. Better yet, find role models and mentors to help you along when things get tough.

4. Relax. Lighten up. Don't take yourself too seriously. Laugh more at yourself and with others. Have more good, clean fun.

5. Give to people much more than you expect to receive from them.

6. Pray to God over each of your decisions, so you will learn to focus on the bigger picture of why you were born, rather than on your desires all the time. When you do find your *thing*, get involved in it immediately. It will help you stay out of trouble.

7. Manage your time and money wisely. Get help on this as needed.

8. Reward yourself for small jobs well done. Congratulate yourself if you even come close to contributing something to your family or society. Be kind to yourself in words and actions when you succeed or fail.

9. Be aware of your fear of success and your fear of failure. Face all your fears and worries; don't panic. If you can't get over your fear, move forward just to spite it.

10. Tell people specifically what you need, want, and expect. People can't read your mind, but often they do want to help you.

These young men had solutions and insights, birthed by street smarts, beyond their years. Chances are good they hadn't read about principles for successful living in any self-help books. They had learned them the hard way—through repeated failure. Not one of them had all the answers that day, but each of them had more than one answer.

The key difference I found between those kids behind bars and those of us who are not locked up is obedience to some basic rules of living. We know that we need to work on our character and that character development is critical to successfully completing God's will for our lives. However, those who are not passionate about pursuing God's plan merely talk about, rather than act on, the "Principles for Living a Better Life." Women who are on-track to pursue their life purpose make changes. They seek to follow the guidelines that will make them better vessels for God's use. They repent and invite God to prune weaknesses, stumbling blocks, and sins from their lives. This intentional discipline helps keep them free of excess baggage, garbage, and excuses for living poorly. It helps set them free to live a better life.

Repentance, a Liberating Step

Repentance is one of the most liberating steps we can take in life, and it comes with so many benefits. When we confess and repent of our sin, we are forgiven and restored. Repentance delivers us from shame, guilt, anger, hopelessness, and bitterness. It releases us from slavery to sin and holds us captive to the desire for a deeper relationship with God. It sets us free to work in concert with God instead of against him, and it allows us to receive the best that God has so graciously planned for our lives.

Repentance also allows us to mitigate, to the best of our ability, the harmful consequences of our sinful actions. Although the list of those we have hurt by our sins may or may not be lengthy, it is a tremendous gift if even one relationship is healed by our repentance. Furthermore, when we prayerfully reflect on repentance and making amends, we are less inclined to sin. Why? Because we will be very busy making things right by restoring our relationship with God, regaining broken trust, guarding against anything that would harm our love for God, and aspiring to holiness.[2]

When we act purposefully and diligently in response to God's command to repent, the limelight shifts quickly to the liberating flip side of each sin. For example, instead of haranguing yourself about your impatience, you can acknowledge the progress you've made when you are patient. Instead of worrying about how prideful you are, you can begin to practice humility. Instead of hating yourself for stealing, you can choose to be deliberately generous. Instead of feeling defeated by your complaining and gossiping, you can choose to think of blessings and encouragement to share with others. Instead of getting depressed about lying and cheating, you can ask God to help you live with integrity and authenticity. Repentance sets you free to focus on your spiritual progress, slow as it might be, rather than on your failures.

So what about you? Are you craving freedom from the things that keep you from living the life you were meant to live? Then, make a list of your stumbling blocks and sins, offer your list to God, and be willing to run from those temptations in the future.

DEALING WITH SINS THAT INTERFERE WITH LIFE PURPOSE

One stumbling block that can hold us back from pursuing our life purpose is pride. Make no mistake about what we are to do with our pride. God expects us to deal with all forms of conceit and arrogance, including the pretense of false humility (which is being proud of our humility!). Warnings against the sin of pride are scattered throughout the Bible: "Pride goes before destruction, and a haughty spirit before a fall;"[3] "The LORD detests all the proud of heart. Be sure of this: They will not go unpunished."[4] So whenever we find ourselves coveting attention, kudos, or recognition, we need to let God deal with our prideful spirit.

I had to learn this lesson the hard way. I was invited to give an eight-minute testimony at my church, and I had asked the Holy Spirit to accomplish his work through me. But a few days after receiving all the thank-yous from sweet members of the congregation, I said to a friend: "I so relished the compliments that I am afraid I let God slip into the background. My attitude became 'Me, me, me! God, see me ride my tricycle.'"

> *If you are all wrapped up in yourself, you are way overdressed.*
> JANE ANN CLARK

She replied, "Perhaps you did attempt to rob God of some of his glory, but his mercies are new every morning. I, too, want to know when I am going to grow out of getting puffed up about God's accomplishments through me. I feel like Bill Murray's character in the movie *Groundhog Day*, who had to keep living the same day again and again. I keep repeating the same scenarios involving ego. Let's agree to hold each other accountable on this."

To this day, I am grateful for that accountability. God knew that I had prayed for a clean heart and was ready for a more disciplined lesson about who was going to get the glory. Shortly after that conversation, I came across the following rarely quoted Bible passage about how King Herod died. It horrified me and reconfirmed that I wanted freedom from the sin of pride:

> An appointment with Herod was granted, and when the day arrived he [Herod] put on his royal robes, sat on his throne and made a speech to them. At its conclusion the people gave him a great ovation, shouting, "It is the voice of a god and not of a man!" Instantly, an angel of the Lord struck Herod with a sickness so that he was filled with maggots and died—because he accepted the people's worship instead of giving the glory to God.[5]

Later, I found a similar story about Uzziah, a powerful king of Judah. Because of his pride, God struck him with leprosy, causing him to live in isolation for the rest of his life.[6] These examples convinced me that God abhors pride. I can only imagine what a disgusting sight it must be in his eyes.

FATHER, FORGIVE ME

Over the years, I have had a great deal of difficulty confessing and repenting of such sins as pride, impatience, cursing, lying, gossiping, manipulating, stealing, raging, being greedy, and excessive drinking. (Yeah, sweet little me!) None of the ugliness of my sins disappeared because I powered up and was able to reject it on my own. Instead, in each situation, God's grace made him willing to swoop down and rescue me again and again from my sinful self.

In some cases, God allowed me to experience a painful or embarrassing consequence that caused me to turn away from a certain destructive habit. In several instances, he gave me new insight from my own life or the life of someone else that removed my desire for a particular sin.

In other cases, he gave me a higher calling, a noble reason that I couldn't ignore, for example, to mothering, to a ministry leadership position, or to a healthier lifestyle. And at times he has simply increased my trust, obedience, or love.

It is astounding how many different ways God can work once we confess and repent. We can be set free from one bad habit after another. Repentance can become such a fast-paced, life-changing expedition that once you get on a roll you won't remember how you got from point "A" to "B" to "C" unless you keep a written record of the key turning points. For example, I found in my journal some long-forgotten thoughts about two of my sins, cursing and stealing. Let me set the stage for each.

The desire to stop cursing grew slowly in my heart. I had dropped several hints to a friend that I was becoming uncomfortable with her "cussing like a drunken sailor," but my milquetoast pleas had no impact. One day I became so sad over that particular sin in my own life that I decided I must walk away from the friendship that encouraged it. I prayed for courage to repent and do what needed to be done when I wrote:

> Lord, you have shown me lately what a poor representative of you I am when I use cuss words. And you have even given me a huge ache in my heart now when X takes your name in vain. I have always felt uncomfortable with that, but now I hate it with a passion. I ask you for the courage to speak up more boldly or walk away from that friendship. All of a sudden, I am truly sorry for my foul mouth. I don't want to curse anymore or be around those who do so. Please give me the help I need to change.

On a different occasion, I came face-to-face with another sin in my life when I asked a friend to call me long distance to chat during work hours. She told me that she felt uncomfortable calling from her place of employment because that would be stealing from her company. Even more important to her than the cost of the call was the time off-task.

So many times you will see people wringing their hands, and saying, "I want to know what my Mission in life is," all the while they are cutting people off on the highway, refusing to give time to people, punishing their mate for having hurt their feelings, and lying about what they did. And it will seem to you that the angels must laugh to see this spectacle. For these people wringing their hands, their Mission was right there, on the freeway, in the interruption, in the hurt, and at the confrontation.[7]
RICHARD NELSON
BOLLES

After I laughed out loud at what I thought to be a ludicrous comment about a silly phone call, my friend explained that she and her husband always discussed the ethics of their work behavior. Her husband, a retired Army officer and West Point graduate, would often refer to the honor code he learned as a cadet: A cadet will not lie, cheat or steal, nor tolerate those who do. She said that simple statement constantly challenged both of them to scrutinize their behavior.

With this new viewpoint to consider, my mind began working overtime during the next several months. I started to seriously examine my thinking and behavior. I began asking myself questions about corporate theft, like using the postal meter for mailing personal correspondence or charging a lunch with friends as a business expense. I eventually wrote:

> Lord, I now realize that it is not right to "borrow" office supplies for home use. Please forgive me. I have decided to write a check to Mr. X for supplies I took. This will not be easy for me, but even more humbling is that I need to ask him for forgiveness. I am so sorry. Thank you for using my friend and her husband's influence to change me. Please mold me into being an honorable woman for you.

I had forgotten about these two incidents of confession that led to repentance. I'm glad I kept a record of them, even though they are horribly embarrassing. They help me see the power God has to remove other sins from my life when I ask him to do so. Now I say, "Lord, if you handled my cursing and stealing, you can surely handle this next thing."

And I know there will be "next things" for me, just as there will be for you. Although we may hesitate at first to take the step of repentance, we can also welcome the opportunity because it equips us to move forward toward God's purpose for our lives.

THE SOJOURNER'S GUIDE TO PRACTICING REPENTANCE

Repentance is a practice that will become very familiar to us as we seek to hear from God about the unique purpose he has for each of us. The following suggestions will help you follow through and make great strides on your pathway to purpose.

Turn toward God

Are you stepping toward repentance by saying, "I must admit my sins to God"? If you answered yes, do whatever it takes (pray unceasingly, meditate on God's Word, seek Christian counseling or therapy, do a Bible study, have conversations, read books) to invite God to work. Your Creator loves you and wants you to succeed on your life mission. Turn toward him and ask him to lead you to a Scripture, person, circumstance, or activity that will help you change your ways.

Memorize a Scripture

You may want to memorize Romans 7:18, one of the most comforting Scripture passages on repentance: "I have the desire to do what is good, but I cannot carry it out." How true this has been in my life! I don't offer this as an excuse to keep sinning but as a reminder to be patient with yourself. God knows how hard it is to change sin patterns. Just remember: you are responding to a God who loves you very much, not to a God who is angry with you for not being able to get it right the first time.

Consider the Consequences of Your Sin

The consequences of your sin can be widespread, including the loss of your career, marriage, family, possessions, education, reputation, self-esteem, passion, or hope, just to name a few. The consequences can even spill over onto the next generation, such as when someone who emulates you is unable to break a sin cycle of abuse or addiction.

Think for a moment about one confessed sin in your life. What were the positive results (obvious or hidden) of repenting of that sin? Now think of a current sin from which you have not repented. What might be the possible negative consequences of it? Ask God today to forgive you for that sin and free you from its power. Don't ask simply to avoid the potentially tough consequences, but ask for forgiveness because God is almighty, and he is waiting for you to repent.

> But he said to me, "My grace is sufficient for you, for my power is made perfect in weakness." Therefore I will boast all the more gladly about my weaknesses, so that Christ's power may rest on me.
> (2 CORINTHIANS 12:9)

Consider Missed Blessings

Sin also can cause you to miss out on blessings such as deeper relationships, joy, peace, a leadership role, good health, intimacy with God, spiritual growth, character development, or financial stability. Recall a past sin and ask yourself, "What blessing might I have missed because of it?" Then, think of a current sin from which you have not repented and identify what the potential missed blessings might be.

Accept Reproof

Ask the Holy Spirit to alert you to your sins and to prepare your heart to hear and accept reproof or correction. That reproof may be delivered unexpectedly by a friend during a conversation or straight from God's heart to yours during a time of planned solitude and silence. In response to this prompt to stop sinning, flee from one temptation this week. Don't apologize to anyone about running away from the temptation, and don't look back—just run!

Be Honest with Yourself about Five Sins

Use the "Five Sins That Distract You from God's Best for Your Life" (below) to identify some of your sin tendencies and evaluate your readiness to carry out God's will for your life. This exercise will help you see the truth about whether or not you are cooperating with God's plan to the fullest. Enlist the help of an objective friend as needed.

FIVE SINS THAT DISTRACT YOU FROM GOD'S BEST FOR YOUR LIFE

1. **Jealousy:** Are you jealous of your neighbor's windfall or of your friend who has such an adoring husband? Are you jealous of the size or scope of someone else's life mission?

2. **Anger:** Are you angry about an illness, a divorce, or an injustice? Are you angry about not knowing what God wants of you? Are you angry with people who are interfering with your God-given vision?

3. **Pride:** Do you like to call attention to your accomplishments? Do you brag about your purposeful assignment? Do you fight God for control of the direction you will take?

4. **Disobedience:** Do you turn a deaf ear to the needy? Are you too busy to pray? Do you neglect your family to carry out your unique life purpose?

5. **Dishonesty:** Do you lie, cheat, or steal? Do you renege on financial obligations in order to fund your kingdom-building dream?

Pray This Prayer

As you pray the following prayer, take a step of faith and ask Jesus to help you. Ask him to take you from where you are today to where he wants you to be.

Dear Jesus, I gratefully

Give you my . . .	**I pray for your . . .**
pride and ego	*humility*
impatience	*patience*
despair	*hope*
anger	*joy*
temper	*kindness*
lies	*truth*
control	*serenity*
doubt	*faith*
discouragement	*perseverance*

Lord, I know that because I'm human, I will still continue to sin, but please reduce the time it takes me to recognize and repent of sins like anger, discouragement, doubt, or greed. If it used to take me a week to recognize and repent of a sin, let it take me one day, one hour, one minute, or one second instead. I don't want my sin to cause me to offend you or rob you of my obedience. Please strengthen me now. In Jesus' precious name I pray. Amen.

RECOMMENDED BOOKS ON CHANGING YOUR WAYS

Make Anger Your Ally, by Neil Clark Warren[8]
Lord, Change Me, by Evelyn Christenson[9]
Breaking Free, by Beth Moore[10]

NOW IS THE TIME TO REPENT

Will you take this next step toward God and his purpose for your life: *to repent and turn away from all your offenses?* If your answer is yes, take heart because as difficult as this step is, it leads to great rejoicing. In fact, Scripture tells us that the angels in heaven rejoice when even one sinner repents![11] And the apostle Paul writes: "Now I rejoice, *not* that you were made sorry, but that your sorrow led to repentance."[12] So as you offer your sins to God, let someone you trust walk alongside you, encourage you, and rejoice with you.

Will you let go of sinful habits that are controlling your life and keeping you prisoner? Will you tell someone about your decision to repent? Are you ready to be set free to become God's woman of character, a woman eager to repent of every sin that would turn her heart away from God and away from fulfilling her purpose on earth? Then go ahead, take the step, repent of your sins. He is waiting for you.

GOD'S WISDOM FOR THE PATHWAY

THE "SAMARITAN WOMAN'S" STEP OF LIFE: REPENTING AND TURNING AWAY FROM ALL YOUR OFFENSES

For a lesson from the nameless Samaritan woman on taking a step toward repentance, read John 4:7–42. Jesus spoke with her when she went to draw water from a well. He told her that he knew she had had five husbands and was now with a man who was not her husband. After he revealed himself to her as the Messiah of the world, she became an evangelist, pointing those in her town to Jesus.

Your repentance over sin may or may not involve a dramatic conversion like the woman at the well, but what sin or character issue are you struggling with? Will you repent now and turn away from your offense?

Personal Pathway Questions

1. How often do you confess your sins to God?

2. Write anything that prompts you to repent. Here are some examples:

   ▰ Knowing that Jesus has forgiven me

   ▰ Reproof or correction from someone I trust and love

   ▰ A Scripture verse that speaks to my heart

   ▰ A book that explains why I am attracted to a particular sin and how to avoid it

   ▰ Getting caught; being embarrassed

   ▰ Focusing on the "flip side" of the sin (for example: humility, integrity, encouragement)

   ▰ Seeing the ugliness of a specific sin in someone else's life

3. Which ideas from Question 2 will you use now to increase your desire to confess and repent?

4. What is God nudging you to do about offering one particular weakness to him?

5. What is your response to this verse? "Let us throw off everything that hinders and the sin that so easily entangles, and let us run with perseverance the race marked out for us" (Hebrews 12:1).

NOTES

1. (p. 99) See Ephesians 4:19–5:21.
2. (p. 102) See 2 Corinthians 7:10–11.
3. (p. 103) Proverbs 16:18, NKJV.
4. (p. 103) Proverbs 16:5.
5. (p. 104) Acts 12:21–23, TLB.
6. (p. 104) See 2 Chronicles 26:1–21.
7. (p. 106) Richard Nelson Bolles, *What Color Is Your Parachute?* (Berkeley, Calif.: Ten Speed Press, 1995, updated annually), 457. Reprinted with permission. Copyright © 1995 by Richard Nelson Bolles, Ten Speed Press, P.O. Box 7123, Berkeley, CA 94707. Available from your local bookseller, by calling 800-841-2665, or visiting www.tenspeed.com.
8. (p. 110) Neil Clark Warren, *Make Anger Your Ally* (Colorado Springs: Focus on the Family, 1990).
9. (p. 110) Evelyn Christenson, *Lord, Change Me*, reprint ed. (Colorado Springs: Chariot Victor Publishing, 1993).
10. (p. 110) Beth Moore, *Breaking Free* (Nashville: Broadman and Holman, 2000).
11. (p. 111) See Luke 15:7, 10.
12. (p. 111) 2 Corinthians 7:9, NKJV (italics added).

Part Four

Go the
Extra Mile

God's *Ministry* Purpose for You:
To Serve Others

Chapter 7

WASH ONE ANOTHER'S FEET

"Now that I, your Lord and Teacher, have washed your feet,
you also should wash one another's feet. I have set you an example
that you should do as I have done for you. . . . Now that you know
these things, you will be blessed if you do them."
(JOHN 13:14–15, 17)

I hope you are eager to take your next step toward discovering God's unique purpose for your life. Although repentance may have been challenging for you, it was necessary to begin to overcome those challenges because the step you are about to take raises the bar another mark or two. But don't be intimidated, the journey thus far has prepared you well. So let's press on and see where God will lead.

The stepping-stone, *wash one another's feet*, sends some of us into a crying, whining fit. At first glance, we sit right down on the nearest rock in the stream and refuse to engage in any such activity. We've been heard to mutter, "I DON'T think so! It's not gonna happen." If you have any such inclination, I'd like you to remember one undeniable fact: Jesus was serious about his followers serving one another, so serious that he washed his disciples' feet.[1]

I don't know if you have noticed, but Jesus frequently set a personal example of the things he most wants us to internalize and emulate. For instance, he showed us how to find peace when he went off alone to pray and listen to his Father (see chapter five). He showed us what a surrendered life looks like when he cried out to his Father in the garden of Gethsemane, "Yet not as I will, but as you will"[2] (more on this in chapter ten). So we would be foolish to ignore the servant example of Jesus. As our role model, he provides the highest level of inspiration to get us off our haunches. He clearly teaches that humble service is a requirement of faith in action.

No matter how much we complain about the high expectations of this servant's step, God has never chosen to recall this stepping-stone. Its rough spots and cracks may not appeal to us, but in God's eyes this stone is beautiful. He will not send it back to the factory for refurbishment. Humble service may not make our priority list, it may not be popular with the masses, but it is what God desires.

A REQUIREMENT WITH RICH REWARDS

I know that serving others will give us a few "What am I doing here?" or "Help! Get me out of here!" moments. I've had some of those myself. But serving others is also very satisfying and rewarding. Although some service tasks may cause a woman to cringe, I've observed that women seem naturally inclined to spend themselves on others. A woman with no desire to help others is as unusual as a woman without a hankering for chocolate or some other forbidden food! So, confidentially, have you dared to ask what you may receive when you serve others? Let's take a look.

Washing one another's feet gives us a mini-purpose for today. I wish I had known this years ago. As I mentioned in chapter three, simply knowing that the small acts of service I was pouring my life into truly mattered to God would have been a hyperlink to hope! The knowledge that those seemingly insignificant acts were part of God's plan for me would have pulled me through many bouts of vague discouragement regarding my life's value and journey.

In addition, humble service in daily things quite often leads to service in a broader arena. No service, no matter how insignificant we may consider it, goes unnoticed or unappreciated by God. I have heard countless stories about how God worked mightily to enlarge the influence and ministries of faithful servants who obeyed him. Those are the saints to whom he entrusts tasks that require even greater obedience. Those are the folks God loves to honor because they follow his lead in wanting not "to be served, but to serve."[3]

Faithful service also yields the reward of learning empathy and patience as you move toward fulfilling your life purpose. Even if that were the only benefit of this step, it would be well worth it. But there is an even greater incentive, and that is the privilege of learning more about and drawing closer to the God we serve.

Watch to see where God is at work and join him![4]
HENRY BLACKABY
AND CLAUDE KING

As you partner with God in serving others, you'll learn to depend on him as the source and strength behind your particular assignments and giftedness. And, because you will be walking in the ministry footsteps of Jesus, you will become more like him. You will be putting into practice what he teaches through his Word. You will experience the joy of standing steadfastly on this stone and ministering in whatever way God asks.

DON'T BE AFRAID OF YOUR FALTERING STEPS

God's goal is for us to become selfless, obedient servants, willing to serve at any time, in any place, and on any assignment. Some of those assignments may be a perfect fit. Others may be inconvenient or cause us to feel uncomfortable. But God wants us to serve him wholeheartedly, no matter what the task. Of course he does not expect us to start with that attitude as new Christians, but he does expect us to grow into it as maturing believers.

I am so grateful that God graciously accepts our honest efforts toward serving others because I have had many faltering steps in this particular part of the stream. I am thankful that he does not view me as an embarrassment even though some of my steps have embarrassed me.

One misguided step occurred when a friend confessed to me, "I feel as if I have sprouted into an unsightly, good-for-nothing, Christian weed. I can't seem to settle into a ministry I like." My initial response was empathic sadness for her, but at the same time, the unpleasant taste of sneaky pride rose up in my throat. I have to admit that inside me was a smug, self-congratulating attitude that I—even as a child—had always had a heart for helping people.

Fortunately, God was gracious to me. He quickly brought to mind how rough my transition into formal church ministry and mission opportunities had been. For some reason, it took a giant leap for me to move from being a grateful believer, focused on personal growth and holiness, to a servant believer, focused on becoming God's hands and feet to others. I remembered how gangly and wilted I felt during that time.

I remember well the emotions I experienced when I was coerced into my first-ever lay ministry role as a Sunday morning greeter. Those painful feelings can best be compared to a camping trip I once took. If you happen to love a rugged camping experience in a tiny tent by an icy stream, please forgive me because I loathe it. My idea of *roughing it* is a hotel without room service.

Despite my personal aversion to camping, I once agreed to go because my husband laid a guilt trip on me. "Your two-year-old son wants you to go on his first campout," he begged. Even I couldn't resist. I survived the treacherous mountain drive, the swarming bees, the invading ants, the horrible horseflies, and the burned food. However, when our German shepherd mutt momentarily mistook my foot for a fish in the stream, I was done. I hollered without hesitation, "Get me out of here. Take me to the Hilton now. I don't care what my son wants!"

I was no more suited for being a Sunday morning greeter than I was for camping. Both activities made me tense, and I decided that no one should be expected to minister or vacation with her stomach tied in knots. God had many servants with a huge heart for welcoming visitors to church, just as he had many happy campers. Whether it was God's logic or my excuse to avoid serving outside my comfort zone, I began looking for ministry opportunities elsewhere.

The surprising thing is that God can use any service adventure, easy or difficult, to help us recognize our need for spiritual maturity. And if we are ever to fulfill and relish our God-ordained purposes in life, we must mature spiritually. That's why the stepping-stone of serving others is so important.

You see, our goal in serving others is to bring glory to God, and as we pursue that goal, our yearning to develop a servant's humble heart and to grow spiritually increases. As we grow spiritually, we bring more glory to God more often, which helps us see the value of pursuing the disciplines that lead to spiritual maturity—having a quiet time, reading Scripture, fasting, tithing, and the like. In turn, pursuing these disciplines feeds our yearning to grow and mature. So our steps toward serving others, however wavering they may be at first, are crucial to our becoming women of purpose. Once we make the commitment to serve, a whole cycle of growth can begin!

OBEDIENCE TESTING 101

Sometimes God may nudge us to serve in an area of our preference because he wants us to get used to the idea of ministering to others. He may give us the option of moving in and out of service opportunities of our own choosing. This allows us to discover for ourselves the ministries we prefer and those for which we are best equipped. We might try hospital visitation, meals ministry, church office volunteering, prison evangelism, and so on. Before long, we will find ministries that match our passions. We will realize that it is a treat and a privilege to serve. We will grow and flourish like a plant in the right soil under the right conditions.

Over the years, I've done my fair share of investigating and trying out ministry opportunities. I noticed that the choir director, for one, cringed when he saw me coming. Was it because I couldn't carry a tune or that I talked too much during rehearsals? I also learned that I could live forever without joining the highly respected hospice care group (too sad for me) and that the church was better off if I stayed away from the tithe counting ministry (too exact for me). And I don't know what I could have offered to the Christmas pageant planning committee (too artistic for me).

> *"I will only reveal myself to those who love me and obey me. The Father will love them too, and we will come to them and live with them. Anyone who doesn't obey me doesn't love me."*
> (JOHN 14:23–24, TLB)

The process of trying out different ministries while seeking to find my niche helped me realize that I love interviewing, life purpose coaching, writing, and teaching. So it is no surprise that for years I was a ministry interviewer who helped other women in our church pinpoint the area of ministry in which they felt God leading them to serve. In time, I also helped write an early version of the train-the-trainer curriculum for that program, which taught others how to conduct the interviews.

I had passed the first test! I had obediently taken the steps to find a ministry in which I liked serving. But who wants to minister only in self-pleasing areas in which we feel comfortable and well-suited? Not I, and I don't think you do either. Spiritual sissies we are not! So the next step is to brace ourselves for a more advanced obedience test.

OBEDIENCE TESTING—THE GRADUATE COURSE

Sometimes God asks us to serve in an assignment that is way outside our comfort zone or area of giftedness. He may do this to stretch our faith or to teach us a valuable lesson. In all honesty, servanthood assignments of this type still sound as awful to me as "Please, let's go camping!" They can trigger a "Poor me!" feeling of personal martyrdom. For that response, I repent each time, knowing that if I care deeply about what my Father wants of me, there is no room for self-pity.

During my trip to Calcutta, God gave me one of those odd, it's-not-my-thing assignments. Those who watched me try to squirm out of the situation said my furrowed brow and stricken face spoke volumes about my discontent.

As only God could have arranged it, my mother and I found ourselves volunteering in the Home for Mentally Ill Women, truly a place for society's outcasts. After serving a lunch of milk, fruit, and mush to the women who had been rescued from the streets, I was asked to entertain them and help them get some exercise. With great enthusiasm, I taught the patients my version of the Irish jig, which was a lively mix of polka and cancan dancing. So far, so good.

Then one of the missionaries handed me a fingernail clipper and asked me to clip the patients' fingernails. Hesitantly, I tried to brace myself with confidence-producing thoughts like *No problem; I can handle this.* Desperate to compare my assigned duty with what my mom was doing, I sneaked a peek at her and quickly became jealous because her task was easier than mine. She had been put in charge of exercising the patients' arms. I silently speculated, *Hmm, maybe she'll trade jobs with me.*

At that moment, though, I noticed a festering sore on the arm of her patient. Within seconds, I decided I'd be much better at trimming unkempt fingernails than dealing with a nasty infection. So I gratefully "clipped away," while my mom found a nurse to help dress her patient's wound.

I was doing my job somewhat reluctantly when, all of a sudden, a patient plopped her foot on my lap, anticipating a pedicure. It was a particularly wide foot, or perhaps my bulging eyes made it appear wider than it was! It was all cracked and blackened from not having worn shoes in years. I looked up at the woman's dark, pixie face and tooth-less grin and recognized her as the one person with whom I had closely bonded that afternoon. In fact, she had sung to me—in English—Frank Sinatra's "It's Now or Never." Was this God's sense of humor? Was it now or never for me to learn to serve wherever he asks?

I closed my eyes to draw on whatever inner strength I had, and something remarkable happened. I saw an image of Jesus washing his disciples' feet, and I felt God was prompting me to do the same for this woman. I eagerly looked around for water, because I would have used it gladly for the sake of obeying *and* having a clean foot on my skirt, but I couldn't find even a cupful anywhere. So I braced myself and began clipping her toenails. I was soon pleasantly surprised when I caught myself playing "This little piggy went to market" on her toes.

I was quite proud of myself for obeying, almost immediately, in what I considered to be an unpleasant situation and was amazed by the grat-itude I saw in the woman's eyes. I realized that not only had God filled her with laughter through me, but that he had somehow allowed me to experience joy through service to her. Was this his way of giving me a glimpse of what Mother Teresa had described when she told me that her work in the slums was pure joy? I made a mental note to spend some time think-ing about that when I was comfortably settled back home, getting my own pedicure. For now, I thought it best to just keep breathing and clipping.

> *You can do no great things—only small things with great love.*[5]
> MOTHER TERESA

I finished clipping the patient's toenails and, with feelings of relief and satisfaction, looked up. I then gasped in horror at the endless line of giggling clientele who hoped I would make time for them as well. I tapped hard on my watch, but it was nowhere near the ladies' after-noon naptime. I mumbled under my breath, "Look, God, I agreed, under pressure, to clip one woman's toenails today! In fact, you tricked me into thinking that it was an easy foot-washing assignment. You don't really think that I, a yuppie, have the type of selfless love it takes to give pedicures to all of these mentally ill women?"

My head reeled with visions of dirty toenails surrounding me, rather than daughters of the King blessing me with their laughter and gratitude. I temporarily lost sight of how my King would be glorified by my obedience. As my panic simmered down, I realized that this needed to be a disciplined afternoon of obedience and silently praying, "Master, because you say so." Simon Peter had spoken those very words to Jesus once, and Jesus had certainly blessed him.

> Simon answered, "Master, we've worked hard all night and haven't caught anything. But because you say so, I will let down the nets." When they had done so, they caught such a large number of fish that their nets began to break. (Luke 5:5–6)

After a while I prayed words of my own:

> Lord, I don't want to simply endure the ministry moments you have scheduled for me today. When you arrange divine service appointments for me, I want to be your hands and feet. Teach me to be a vessel for you. Help me to be willing always to handle the task-at-hand, whether in my home, church, community, or mission field. Remind me that to live for you is to serve others, and that to serve others is to really live.

The more I prayed, the more I could feel God ministering to me and through me. He was making me calmly sufficient to serve the basic human needs of my sisters in Christ.

So what about you? Perhaps nobody is going to ask you to wash feet or clip toenails in the near future, but are you ready to go all-out and serve in whatever capacity God wants? When my children were young, I told them that obedience was doing what they were told, doing it with a positive attitude, and doing it immediately. As they were growing up, I congratulated them if they got even one or two of those elements correct. But if they got all three—that was an obedience home run!

It is the same for us as we serve our Lord. He expects cheerful, prompt obedience. Jesus said, "You are my friends if you do what I command."[6] I agree that it is often hard to follow God's instructions, and I know that we are merely human and will fail sometimes in our efforts to become faithful servants. But let's help each other remember that serving others is an act of obedience to the one who paid for our every act of disobedience by his death on the cross.

THE SOJOURNER'S GUIDE TO FOOT WASHING

The following suggestions will help you discover opportunities to obey God's leading as he directs your path of serving others. Take as much time on this step as you need until washing the feet of others or ministering to them in some other way becomes a natural part of your everyday life. I'm still plugging along, day by day.

Seize an Opportunity to Give Yourself Away Today

Ask God what opportunity he would like you to seize today to give yourself (your energy, time, and/or resources) away. Then volunteer for the next service moment he puts in your pathway. Whether it is logical or not, whether it is convenient or not, pitch in and serve where God is busy. Frequent, humble service experiences, which are steeped in lessons of trust in God, are a training ground for his future ministry and mission plans for you. Tell God you want him to use you—whenever, wherever, and however—and see where the adventure takes you!

Think Long Term

What is God leading you to do for him long term? Does he want you to join the benevolence team at your church, go on a mission trip, or help start a church? Whether God reveals a suggestion that takes you into your local community or around the world, consider a long-term ministry perspective that will impact your service commitment forever.

Only a life lived for others is worthwhile.
ALBERT EINSTEIN

Stay Balanced; Retain Some Margin

During this step, be aware of your Plimsoll mark! No, a Plimsoll mark is not a sophisticated theological term; it is the load-limit line that the English Parliament mandated be drawn on the hull of merchant ships because too often they were being overloaded and sinking under their own weight. So, be aware of your limits. Don't overload your schedule with service commitments that exceed the healthy limitations of your life.

By the way, you are the only one who can keep your service ship from sinking. Do not expect anyone—not Congress, your church, or your family—to prevent you from carrying too heavy a load. On the other hand, don't hide behind self-created busyness as an excuse not to serve. Discard everything that could distract you from a course of service.

Take a Test

Take a spiritual gifts inventory to see if you can identify your top three spiritual gifts. Then, spend some time investigating and reflecting on the possible applications of those gifts. For example, if your gift is administration, would it be a good fit for you to serve on the church retreat committee? If your gift is mercy, what opportunities to visit the sick and infirm are available to you? Then, make up your mind to experiment with what you've learned. You may find my "Recommended Books" to be helpful in this part of the process.

RECOMMENDED BOOKS ON SPIRITUAL GIFTS FOR MINISTRY

Discovering Your Spiritual Gifts: A Personal Inventory Method,
by Kenneth Kinghorn[7]
CLASS 301: Discovering My Ministry, Saddleback Church[8]

Try on New Ministry Shoes

Maybe you already know how God wired you. You've taken a spiritual gifts assessment test or a personality profile, and you're sure God has given you a glimpse of how he wants you to use your gifts, personality, abilities, passion, and experiences. That's great! But don't let your discovery journey end there. You'll never really know where God wants you to serve until you try on a variety of opportunities.

When my daughter first learned to walk, she headed straight to my closet to try on my shoes. For years she could be seen clomping around the house in mismatched shoes. In the morning I might see her in a high heel and a tennis shoe. Later in the afternoon she might be wearing a house slipper and a sandal. Trying on shoes is comical when it is child's play, but the concept of trying on lots of giftedness shoes to see which ones God designed for you to wear can be helpful to an adult.

So, take a look in God's ministry closet. Go ahead, try on the shoes! Clomp around some. Give yourself permission to fall down. You'll need to practice walking through some anxiety or uncertainty, which will help you develop new skills and insights. In time, you'll learn to recognize whether or not certain ministry shoes are a good or perfect fit.

Now Is the Time to Serve Others in Jesus' Name

Will you take this next step toward God and his purpose for your life of *washing one another's feet*? God is calling you to serve him. Have you put aside your personal preferences and made yourself available to him in the arenas in which he is working in a mighty way? Do you seize opportunities to give yourself away?

Whether you are currently comfortable in a ministry or not, consider how God might be able to use you in a tough, temporary, assignment either at home or overseas. Run toward whatever he shows you. And, in moments of extreme obedience, do as my mentor, Ina, suggests: "Kneel at the foot of the cross to pray for strength and joy."

Nothing in this world compares to the joy of being used by God. Being an instrument in his hands gives you a deeper awareness of who he is and the purpose he has for your life. Faithful service often results in God trusting you with more vision for your life and inviting you to be part of his bigger plan.

Our job during this step is simple: do less talking about service and more serving. May this be the prayer of your heart:

> *God, help me learn to wash others' feet joyfully and promptly or serve them well in any other way you ask of me. I want to stay in each particular ministry only as long as you want me in it. In your good timing and wisdom, nudge me to seek out new, bold ways to serve you.*

If you want to become God's woman of service, don't delay. Press on.

GOD'S WISDOM FOR THE PATHWAY

THE "DORCAS" STEP OF LIFE: WASHING ONE ANOTHER'S FEET

For a lesson from Dorcas, beloved servant to her friends, read Acts 9:36-42. Mourners packed into a room to grieve the loss of Dorcas when she died. She was a kind woman who had made a great impact on her community by her gift of *helps*.

What legacy of unselfish service will you leave? Will you follow where God is leading you today? If yes, whisper that as a prayer. You may also want to use the prayer below:

Lord, I know that service is a disposition—an attitude of my heart, an availability of my spirit. When I allow you to empty my heart of selfish pride, I make room for you to enter. Though you are rich, you willingly emptied yourself out of love for me, becoming a humble servant. Help me become more like you.

Personal Pathway Questions

1. In what ways do you typically submit to God's plan of service each day?

2. What holds you back from acts of service? What solution comes to mind to remedy that?

3. List as many of your church, community, and world mission assignments you can remember participating in over the years. Put "LF" by several of your **L**east **F**avorite or "MF" by several of your **M**ost **F**avorite service commitments.

4. What ministry would you like to investigate? Why?

5. What is one step you could take toward service today (for example, make a phone call, do some research on a topic, meet with a ministry leader, take a class, start serving)?

NOTES

1. (p. 117) See John 13:14–17.
2. (p. 118) Matthew 26:39.
3. (p. 119) Matthew 20:28.
4. (p. 119) Henry Blackaby and Claude King, *Experiencing God* (Nashville: Broadman and Holman, 1994), 44. © by Broadman and Holman Publishers. All rights reserved.
5. (p. 124) Quoted in Kathryn Spink, ed., *Life in the Spirit: Reflections, Meditations, Prayers* (San Francisco: Harper and Row, 1983), 45.
6. (p. 126) John 15:14.
7. (p. 127) Kenneth Kinghorn, *Discovering Your Spiritual Gifts: A Personal Inventory Method* (Grand Rapids: Zondervan, 1984).
8. (p. 127) *CLASS 301: Discovering My Ministry*, Saddleback Church (Lake Forest, Calif.: www.pastors.com, 1985).

Chapter 8

WALK WITH INTEGRITY

The integrity of the upright guides them,
but the unfaithful are destroyed by their duplicity.
(PROVERBS 11:3)

Caution ahead! The next stepping-stone in the stream is a wobbly one. It is broad and level on top, but underneath it is uneven and poorly set in the streambed. You will definitely need to pay attention while you maneuver across it because its nickname is *Rocking Horse*, and it is famous for pitching would-be sojourners into the drink. You will need prayer, balance, and concentration to avoid being thrown off this stepping-stone, *walk with integrity, not duplicity.*

Before either of us takes a careless step, let's pause to examine this stone closely. Our integrity determines whether we halfheartedly or fully participate in God's best purposes for our lives. Authentic living with genuine integrity bonds our hearts with the very heart of God. So let's begin by clarifying what we mean by integrity and duplicity.

INTEGRITY VS. DUPLICITY

Integrity can be defined as oneness between our mind and actions, or unity of our thoughts and deeds. A woman of integrity thinks what she says she thinks, feels what she says she feels, and does what she says she will do. She keeps the promises she makes. Her motives are pure. She is honest, upright, and genuine. She is *real* in her relationships.

When one has integrity there is an absence of hypocrisy. He or she is personally reliable, financially accountable, and privately clean . . . innocent of impure motives.[1]
CHARLES SWINDOLL

Duplicity, in contrast, is deliberate deceptiveness. Double-dealing and two-faced, it is the enemy of integrity. A woman of duplicity has the ability, like a seasoned poker player, to convey messages through her words or actions that are opposite of her inner thoughts or planned actions. What is actually in her heart or on her mind would surprise you.

The differences between integrity and duplicity seem pretty clear, don't they? But here's where the wobbly part of this step comes into play. On the surface a woman of integrity and a woman of duplicity may appear the same. The differences are visible only when you take a close look at what's underneath their well-polished veneer. You see the truth only when you evaluate the motives behind their actions.

Let me illustrate what I mean. Consider Jonie, a woman who is an expert at duplicity. She does not want to appear too aggressive or too assertive, but never underestimate her determination to get her way. Jonie doesn't want anything to do with her husband's office friends. So imagine her reaction when the group decides to go out for dinner and bowling, and her husband really wants her to go. Jonie goes through the motions as if she is planning to go. But she holds the trump card because she has "tried and tried," yet just can't find a reliable babysitter. This gives her an admirable, last-minute excuse to bow out. She not only gets her way, but she looks like a dedicated mom as she does it. That's duplicity at its finest!

So What's the Big Deal?

In Jonie's case, her husband may have been disappointed and felt like the odd-man-out, but no one really was harmed by her deception. Everyone had a good time, including Jonie! Of course her husband's colleagues understood that she couldn't leave the children home alone. Sometimes those things just happen. They figure they'll see her the next time, but Jonie is slippery. You and I already know she'll have another excuse that will prevent her from joining them.

So what's the problem? It is simple: God abhors duplicity. God does not want Jonie, nor does he want you or me, to spend our days duping people. The issue is not whether people notice our deception or are harmed by it. The issue is that God wants us to walk in integrity, not duplicity. He wants our actions to be honest and our motives to be pure.

God is all-knowing and everywhere present. No facades or false motives can be hidden from him. He hates it when our secret motive is, for example, to manipulate a situation, control an opinion, seek revenge, stir up trouble, embarrass someone, or show off. Those things are destructive to our relationships with him and with others. God knows that living without integrity leads to cheating, envy, slander, scheming, malice, flattery, treachery, and secret wickedness, which the Bible says inevitably destroy us as well as our relationships. Duplicity and its companions have no place in God's purposes for those who love and serve him.

> *The LORD does not look at the things [woman] looks at. [Woman] looks at the outward appearance, but the LORD looks at the heart.*
> (1 SAMUEL 16:7)

In case you have any doubts about how God views integrity and duplicity, read Jesus' scathing words to some of the highly esteemed members of his community:

"Woe to you, teachers of the law and Pharisees, you hypocrites! You are like whitewashed tombs, which look beautiful on the outside but on the inside are full of dead men's bones and everything unclean. In the same way, on the outside you appear to people as righteous but on the inside you are full of hypocrisy and wickedness."[2]

Do you shiver when you read of Jesus talking like that? I do. I don't know about you, but it makes me appreciate the fact that I was not living in New Testament times when Jesus could publicly expose my impure motives. I am grateful that he exposes my true motives to me in private. I welcome his personal guidance and willingness to help me lead a life of integrity. I don't want to take a false step and be thrown off course in pursuing God's purposes for my life. We can be thankful that God will help each of us become honest, authentic women to whom he can entrust a challenging life mission.

But, as much as we may desire to walk with integrity and pure motives as we pursue our mission, our actual behavior may be quite different. It is disturbing how quickly impure motives can creep in and upset even our most honorable intentions. So let us dig a little deeper and closely examine other aspects of our motives and how those things impact the fulfillment of our life purpose.

GOD SEES THROUGH OUR SELF-SERVING MOTIVES

God is an expert at spotting seemingly innocent yet self-serving motives. These are twisted rationalizations for prideful, lazy, unkind, disobedient, immoral, self-centered, or unethical behavior. Consider the woman who donates money to a worthy cause but does so for personal recognition rather than because her heart's desire is to help others.

Or what about the woman who, in order to get what she wants, begs, "God, if you will please, please, please tell me my grand purpose in life, I promise I will work really hard on it." But God knows that once her curiosity is satisfied and the excitement wanes, she won't follow through on the hard work of completing the mission he crafted for her before she was born. Her true motive was selfish—to feel the thrill of discovering his plan, not to accept the responsibility that came with it.

Impure, self-serving motives displease God and discolor our gifts of service to our family, church, and community. When it comes to such motives, God expresses his displeasure best (here through the words of the prophet Haggai):

> "You people . . . were contaminating your sacrifices by living with self-ish attitudes and evil hearts—and not only your sacrifices, but everything else that you did as a 'service' to me. And so everything you did went wrong."[3]

Don't you think that statement ought to be strong enough to discourage us from being careless about our motives? I surely do! But do you know what? We still, at times, will operate with impure motives. When we do, we can be deeply grateful for God's grace, because often he will forgive us and use us in spite of our failings.

God Can Use Impure Motives

This may come as a shock to you, but God *can* use impure motives. That's right! He has used my daughter's and mine, and he may decide to use yours as well. For example, years ago my daughter Stephanie reluctantly agreed to sing at a senior center only because I insisted she do so. I can't remember if I used the martyred-mother technique of "you owe me" or if I pulled out all the stops with the classic, "No discussion—I'm the Mom" routine. Regardless of which persuasive parental tactic I employed, I poured adequate guilt into her young heart, and off we went.

In spite of my control-driven motivation and Steph's compliance-driven motivation, God still used the experience poignantly. He revealed to her a true desire for using her voice to serve God's people. He gave her a taste of putting love into action and being changed by ministry.

GOD ISN'T INTERESTED IN MINISTRY-BY-GUILT

Ministry-by-guilt is a common motivational misstep that throws many women off balance, and they may not even understand why. How many times, for example, have you served with a fake smile because of the haunting words *should* or *supposed to*? If you hear yourself using those words when you are making a decision, it can be a warning sign that you need to take time out for a motive check.

I have to admit that for many years my driving motive for service was guilt. I tried so hard to live up to the agenda and expectations other people had for me. I worried about what people would say about me if I didn't perform as expected. I found it easier to do a given task, even if I didn't want to, than to spend countless hours feeling guilty for not doing it.

One day I unexpectedly came face to face with my true motive. During a lunchtime prayer meeting at work, I casually said to a friend, "Nick, I know that I *should* teach second grade Sunday school again this year, but honestly I don't want to." I thought for a moment, then continued, "Oh, never mind. I wish I hadn't bothered you with my complaining. I know the church needs me; I guess I'll just do it. It won't kill me."

Nick's kindly spoken admonishment will be engraved in my mind forever: "Please don't do the church any favors. We're not desperate. We want people to serve those thirsty little second graders out of a love for Jesus, not out of guilt. The kids need their bazillion questions answered, noses wiped, and shoes tied by someone who loves being with them and teaching them that Jesus died to save them."

Maybe I had been too busy or too tired from wiping my own kids' noses to realize that I had been begrudgingly doing church ministry out of guilt. Whatever the reason, I knew my friend was right. I was not serving in the way God (or I) wanted. God wanted me to serve him with integrity and pure motives, not out of guilt! When I realized that, I immediately began changing how I approached the ministries God put before me. I began to purge my vocabulary of the "I have to" phrase. Although I still suffer occasionally from the residual effects of having served out of guilt for so many years, I am beginning to understand that God cares deeply about our attitudes and motives. I'm living proof that the battle against impure motives is as tough as the battle of the bulge.

I hope I haven't inadvertently caused any confusion for you. In chapter seven, I did explain the concept of serving God wherever and whenever he calls, but please catch the screaming difference here. By all means try out different areas of ministry, even some you don't think you will like. But if you cannot serve in a particular capacity with the love of Jesus, and the Lord knows you've diligently tried to do so, I beg you to stop before someone gets hurt. It may be time for you to move on and leave the guilt behind. Ministry-by-guilt lacks integrity. It risks damaging your witness of the gospel to those you are serving.

GOD CALLS US TO MORE THAN A HUMAN OBLIGATION

For years every other Thursday night, my son recited the phrase, "to do one's duty to one's country and to obey the Boy Scout law," as part of the pledge at his troop meetings. I heard that pledge for years, and it caused me to grow increasingly curious about why people volunteer. I wondered if they were motivated by duty, obligation, responsibility, or something else.

My curiosity also was piqued because I was meeting more and more good, non-Christian people who volunteered to serve others. Some were motivated to serve because it was the right thing to do, some because they were afraid of bad karma if they didn't, and others just because it made them feel good. So I decided to interview Dr. Roger Sperry, the right brain-left brain theorist and Nobel laureate in Medicine/Physiology. Because he was a renowned humanist, I wanted to know his scientific rationale for why we should serve others.

I hoped he could help me sort through my confusion about the underlying motives for human service.

Chatting with Dr. Sperry was my first encounter, up close and personal, with some of the basic principles of secular humanism. He was deeply concerned that our planet is fairly close to a total breakdown. He considered Earth to be almost uninhabitable from nuclear buildup, population explosion, loss of topsoil, and damage to the rain forests and the ozone layer. He said that caring about what happens to other human beings and meeting their needs must stem from a scientifically based value system in which service is a recipe for survival, dominance, and continuity. In other words, it is our duty to be helpful to others in order to promote the survival of the species and the earth.[4]

As a maturing Christian, I had to carefully sort through what he told me. I knew that many organisms in this world help other members of their species. The honeybee, for example, works endlessly to ensure survival of the hive. The male stickleback fish will go without food, almost to the point of starvation, as he protects the nest and its future-generation occupants. But what about humans? Are we not expected to give beyond the level of other species? And what about Christians? Didn't Jesus give us a specific guidepost for our motive for loving when he preached, "As I have loved you . . . you also love one another"?[5]

Hearing Dr. Sperry verbalize the "scientific" reasons for service made me sensitive to the fact that my motives often had been to satisfy obligations and meet responsibilities rather than to actually show the love of Jesus to others. I was beginning to see that, at times, I had been serving out of a humanistic mindset and motivation although I professed my belief in God, Jesus, and the Holy Spirit. It was an eye-opener for me in terms of examining my motives for service.

MOTIVES UNDER A MAGNIFYING GLASS

How quickly we can stop walking in integrity! At times duplicity is our intent: we know it and we don't care. More often, however, a woman who wants to pursue God's purposes fails to walk with integrity because she is not diligently checking her life for signs of duplicity. She is blissfully unaware of her impure motives.

I often imagine that God is searching the world for women of integrity who will fulfill his purposes for their lives. Almost as if he is holding a magnifying glass, he notices every one of our hypocritical disguises. He sees through every clever deception. He has planned for us a much more honorable and fulfilling life than what he often sees.

As I've said before, God can use the worst of sinners, the most inauthentic of us to accomplish his work. But how he must long to work with women who reflect the purity of his heart. How he must long to be united in purpose with women who speak the truth with their lives.

SELF-TEST FOR WALKING WITH INTEGRITY

So how do we become women of integrity? Most important, integrity requires a willingness to inspect closely the motives for our actions. Is our motive, for example, to impress someone, get sympathy, avoid embarrassment, or make people like us? We need to learn to check our motives for everything we do—from mentoring to committee work, from classroom volunteering to visiting a lonely neighbor. We test our motives by regularly asking one simple question: "Why am I doing this?"

> *All a [woman's] ways seem innocent to [her], but motives are weighed by the LORD.*
> (PROVERBS 16:2)

This process can unleash deep, unsettling questions about our integrity, such as: What's my real motive for wanting God to reveal my unique life purpose—to give me bragging rights? Was gossip the underlying reason for the prayer request I made for my neighbor? Did I use flattery to get my way today? Did I buy that extravagant birthday gift for my child out of guilt for not being home more?

"Whoa! Time out," you say, "I'm not really that bad—am I?" Agreed, you're not, but all of us are susceptible to these motive mistakes that throw us off balance.

By asking the probing—yes, sometimes painful—questions, we learn to be honest with ourselves. As we learn to thoroughly inspect our hearts, we become women of deeper character. When we find areas of duplicity and take steps toward integrity, we deepen our relationship with God, and that is the best way to resume our journey toward purpose.

Of course, there are times when we do *not* need to ask probing questions about our motives—we just do what we need to do simply because it needs to be done. I think chores such as scrubbing toilets, ironing, changing the cat litter box, weeding, or taking out the trash fall into this category. When it is our turn to fulfill this type of responsibility, we can choose to do it lovingly or begrudgingly, but I don't think we need to spend a lot of time pondering our motives related to it!

THE IMPACT OF INTEGRITY

When it is our determined purpose to learn to be women of integrity and pure motives, not only do we begin to think differently, we also will act, talk, pray, and serve in a different manner. A woman of integrity can look herself in the mirror and say, "I am who I say I am." She will be able to hold her head up and look people in the eye. She will have no evil twin lurking in the darkness, ready to lunge forth to take advantage of someone, protect turf, or stage-manage lives. What a feeling of relief and freedom! No more hiding, pretending, or guilt. No more burnout from the exhausting drain of secrecy, hidden motives, vain conceit, selfish ambition, and shame. That peace of mind alone is worth the effort!

As a woman who walks with integrity, you are a role model to your children, friends, neighbors, and others who desperately need examples of authenticity and honesty. The lying, deceit, and hypocrisy will stop with you. You will be the one to explain to your teenager why he should not use his friend for selfish gain. You will have the privilege of advising a friend who is being tempted by a get-rich-quick scheme. You will be a light to some people on your busy ministry team—members who have forgotten that Jesus is the reason they serve.

MY CALCUTTA MOTIVES REVISITED

Recently, as part of my ongoing efforts to walk in integrity with the Lord, I decided to check my deepest underlying motives for having gone to serve in Calcutta. I already knew some of my reasons for going were because I was sad, confused, lonely, bored, and wanted some answers to life's questions. Those things were true, but they weren't the whole truth.

The rest of the truth included what I wrote in my spiritual journal at the time. I wrote that I needed passion, drama, and theatrics in my life. I went, in part, to raise eyebrows back home and to get attention and recognition. I had been ousted from several of my roles that had provided this fodder in my life, and quite frankly, I missed the blood-pumping, heart-thumping stuff. I also wrote that I had gone on that trip with the curious heart of an interviewer, an investigator, an observer—but had convinced myself that I had gone as a selfless missionary.

By clarifying my motives after the fact, I understood why I hadn't been able to do all the work that was there for me to do. My motives hadn't made me the huge Christian failure I came home thinking I was, but they had caused much stress for me and everyone else. I have learned since the critical importance of trying to clarify my motives before I serve.

> *Serve him with wholehearted devotion and with a willing mind, for the LORD searches every heart and understands every motive behind the thoughts.*
> (1 CHRONICLES 28:9)

The Sojourner's Guide to Walking with Integrity

The following suggestions are designed to help you evaluate your integrity and sort out your motives as you seek to discover and fulfill God's purposes in your life. Take whatever time you need to complete each step.

Ask God for a Specific Example

Ask God to show you a specific instance when you were double-minded like Judas, who used a kiss to betray Jesus, or like the Pharisees, who were hypocrites. Will he remind you of a time when you used your sweetest voice on the phone in order to appear likeable but were really furious inside? Will he help you recall your offer to pray for someone so that you could impress others with your holiness? Fasten your seatbelt for this exercise. It could get very rocky.

Then, as when you deal with any other sin, confess it to the Lord and repent. Confessing an impure motive to God can be humiliating if you do not remember his grace, but his grace is always available to you. If you have been living a fragmented life of lies and duplicity, trust that God will rejoice in your willingness to talk to him about it. Let him change you. Let him give you one of his greatest gifts: making you whole again.

Ask a Friend for Specifics

Once you have asked for forgiveness, repentance requires that you set up some boundaries for yourself in this area. Look for one trustworthy, safe individual with whom you feel comfortable talking, one who is willing to discuss this and other issues related to spiritual growth. Schedule at least one lively, unabashed conversation about integrity, authenticity, and duplicity. Discuss in detail some of the motives with which each of you struggle. Get real with your plans to offer your weaknesses to God. Ask him to carve out every bit of duplicity from your lives.

Offer Your Impure Motives to God

Most of my motives could have benefited from a kids' playground rule I once heard: "I get do-overs!" Thankfully, God gives us "do-overs." If you have a favorite unhealthy motive such as pity, profit, or reward, offer that impure motive to God so he can purify it. When you do this, you will be more fully equipped to live out his purposes, and you will be less likely to fulfill his purposes for the wrong reasons.

So let me take the liberty of asking some personal questions in this regard: What is your motive for wanting God to give you an important life purpose? Is it to build up your reputation, feel good about what you are able to accomplish, reduce your loneliness, or satisfy your curiosity? How do your motives compare with God's motives for assigning you a distinct life purpose? Doesn't he do so because he loves you, trusts you, and wants you to become like Jesus? Doesn't he expect the same in return—that you love him, trust him, and want to become like Jesus? Set aside time in your schedule this week to offer God any of your impure motives related to your purpose, ministry, or life mission.

RECOMMENDED BOOKS ON MOTIVES AND INTEGRITY

A Life of Integrity: 12 Outstanding Leaders, Raise the Standard for Today's Christian Men, by Howard Hendricks[6]
The Real Deal Workbook, by Dan Webster[7]

NOW IS THE TIME TO PRACTICE INTEGRITY

Will you take this next step toward God and his purpose for your life, to *walk with integrity, not duplicity?* There is no doubt about it, living a life of integrity and authenticity is hard work. But we cannot begin to imagine how much God looks forward to this step in your life and mine. He loves to use women who lead examined lives.

If no one has ever coached you on integrity and motives, it is reasonable that you may not have addressed them. So, if God has not yet launched you into a bold, inspired assignment, it would be a good idea to check out this area of your life. But please don't be alarmed. There can be many other reasons for a stalled mission. A delay in receiving a vision from God could also be due to your need for skill and relational preparation, to God's perfect timing in your life, or because he is readying the hearts of those he is sending you to serve.

Are you ready to be a godly woman of integrity? Are you eager to weigh the good and evil of your thoughts and actions? Let today be the day you begin to pray about walking with more integrity. Let today be the day you begin to examine your motives more closely. Don't let it end without acknowledging one impure motive to God. Don't put your head on the pillow tonight until you make a commitment to change what you now know needs to be changed. If you do that, I have a feeling you will sigh with relief as you doze off.

GOD'S WISDOM FOR THE PATHWAY

THE "MIRIAM" STEP OF LIFE: WALK WITH INTEGRITY, NOT DUPLICITY

For a lesson of what happened to Miriam, Moses' sister, when she had improper motives, read Numbers 12. Miriam was jealous of Moses' influence and power. God knew that. Instead of being humbly honest with God about her envy, her wounded pride caused her to criticize Moses' wife. Her motives: to discredit Moses and to attempt to feel better about herself by causing people to think less of him. God dealt severely with her jealous, ego-laden efforts to dishonor his chosen messenger.

What is one of your secret, impure motives? If you can't think of any, Psalm 139:23-24 is a good prayer to say to invite God's inspection: "Search me, O God, and know my heart; test me and know my anxious thoughts. See if there is any offensive way in me, and lead me in the way everlasting."

Personal Pathway Questions

1. Think about a time when a lack of integrity led you to cheating, envy, slander, scheming, malice, flattery, treachery, secret wickedness, duplicity, vain conceit, selfish ambition, or some other sin. Talk to God about how you now feel about the situation. Ask him to forgive you, if you have never done so before.

2. Oswald Chambers reminds us to check our motives for doing ministry. He asks if we serve out of our gratitude that Christ died to save us:

   > Have you delivered yourself over to exhaustion because of the way you have been serving God? If so, then renew and rekindle your desires and affections. Examine your reasons for service. Is your source based on your own understanding or is it grounded on the redemption of Jesus Christ?[8]

   What about you? What is your primary reason for service? Give some in-depth thought to why you serve. Think about Jesus' compassion and humility when he served others, but most of all, meditate on his selfless, loving sacrifice on the cross.

3. To begin to live a more authentic life of integrity, take this opportunity to question your motives for any of your routine actions, such as giving a gift, making a prayer request, going to a social gathering, offering to help someone, supporting a cause, giving a speech, volunteering at your church office, or making a large purchase. In your journal or notebook, create a simple chart, like this:

My Pure Motives	**My Impure Motives**

4. What thoughts do you have about your lists in Question 3? Confess any duplicity and pray for God to instill a love for integrity in your heart.

NOTES

1. (p. 132) Charles Swindoll, *Rise and Shine: A Wake-Up Call* (Portland, Ore.: Multnomah, 1989), 190.
2. (p. 134) Matthew 23:27–28.
3. (p. 135) Haggai 2:14–15, TLB.
4. (p. 138) Personal interview with Dr. Sperry at California Institute of Technology, Pasadena, California, 19 October, 1987. (Roger Sperry was Professor Emeritus of Psychobiology and a veteran pioneer in brain research. Dr. Sperry's findings on the two hemispheres of the brain and their respective functions earned him the Nobel Prize in Medicine/Physiology in 1981. His book, *Science and Moral Priority: Merging Mind, Brain, and Human Values*, was published in 1983. He died in 1994.)
5. (p. 138) John 13:34, NKJV.
6. (p. 143) Howard Hendricks, *A Life of Integrity: 12 Outstanding Leaders Raise the Standard for Today's Christian Men* (Sisters, Ore.: Multnomah, 2003).
7. (p. 143) Dan Webster, *The Real Deal Workbook.* Published by Authentic Leadership, Inc., 550 Old Orchard Road, Holland, MI 49423; phone 616-335-8500; www.authenticleadership.com.
8. (p. 145) Taken from *My Utmost for His Highest* by Oswald Chambers, edited by James Reimann, copyright © 1992 by Oswald Chambers Publications Assn., Ltd. Original edition copyright © 1935 by Dodd Mead & Co., renewed 1963 by the Oswald Chambers Publications Assn., Ltd., and is used by permission of Discovery House Publishers, Box 3566, Grand Rapids, MI 49501. All rights reserved.

Part Five

Run to
Jesus

God's *Worship* Purpose for You:
To Magnify Him with Your Life

Chapter 9

EXPECT THE DESIRES OF YOUR HEART

Delight yourself in the LORD and
he will give you the desires of your heart.
(PSALM 37:4)

For many women, our next step will appear to be a welcome relief. You may catch yourself singing a tune and praising God as you touch down on the stepping-stone, *expect God to give you the desires of your heart.* Yet an uneasiness may start to build within you that you don't understand. I have some ideas about what might be happening, so let's take time out to sort through the cause of that unexpected emotional shift before we continue our journey on the pathway to purpose.

This step may uncover some deeply conflicted feelings within you. Do you feel on the one hand that you want to jump onto this stepping-stone and see what wonderful things God has in store for you, yet on the other hand fear you will actually end up quite disappointed? You may feel a rush of excitement at the prospect of being given the desires of your heart but then rationalize it away with the thought, *God probably won't give me what I really want.*

Perhaps you find yourself wondering, *Maybe this stepping-stone isn't really from God. What if it is one of Satan's traps to coax me into wanting worldly rewards? Just in case, maybe I should step on this stone as lightly and quickly as I can—as if it's a hot plate—so I don't get burned.*

You may have other lingering concerns. If you are truly honest with yourself, you may have to admit that your deepest desires have much more to do with your own happiness and security than with God's purposes and your holiness. Or, you may feel that you don't deserve to receive such extravagant rewards in this life.

YOUR PASSION—IT'S A GOD THING

Let me assure you, this stepping-stone is *not* a trap in disguise. This stone truly is as safe as it looks. The psalmist David spells out the win-win nature of this step in Psalm 37:4. I like to explain its general message like this:

If you will make God the chief affection of your inmost heart . . .
Meaning you delight yourself in the Lord, find enormous pleasure and joy in him, get to know him well by continually sitting in his presence and obeying him.

He will give you the desires of your heart.
Meaning you will receive boundless enthusiasm for the deep passions, cravings, longings, petitions, and aspirations that he planted in your heart.

God wants you, his daughter, to have the desires of your heart. (Not the human desires that tempt you to sin,[1] but godly ones.)

Do you have any idea why God wants this for you? It is very simple. He is a passionate God. He has deep, moving desires for his creation, and one of those is a longing for intimacy with you. He created you to be happiest when you are passionate about him, affectionate to him, and bringing glory to him. He placed desires in your heart before you were born—desires for his plans, his purposes, his goals. And he can't wait for you to unwrap that gift!

The life of Jesus, God's perfect son, is a beautiful, real-life example of what God wants for us in life. While Jesus lived on earth, he was a passionate man. He was on fire for his Father's work and captured audiences with his bold, impassioned messages. Everything he did brought glory to God. Many people flocked to him, and his deep, fervent love for them changed their lives.

Can you take the step to see God as your loving Father, your Abba/Pappa, who wants to surprise and delight you with the desires of your heart? I urge you to consider that God is waiting for you to recognize and enjoy the passions he gave you. You will need them on your adventure, both for your times of personal restoration and to accomplish his work. Let's take a peek and see what we find inside the gift box of passions that God has lovingly prepared for each of us.

UNWRAP GOD'S GIFT OF PASSION

Our passion reflects our deepest yearnings. It underscores the beauty we crave, such as art or music, and reflects our need for such intangibles as freedom or adventure. It can be an expression of our most important drives. For example, a passion for detective work or crossword puzzles might be an expression of a drive to solve problems. Passion can be so powerful it seems to have a life of its own. Unbidden, it can lead us to lose ourselves for hours in a fascinating world where time seems to stand still.

> *What do you do so well that you would enjoy doing it without pay? What is your passion, the spark that needs only a little breeze to ignite into a raging fire?*[2]
> BOB BUFORD

So what do the desires of *your* heart look like? Does your greatest passion manifest itself in the form of a hobby such as a love of miniature dollhouses, basketball, horses, or computers? Does it show up in your career through your love of law, sales, medicine, or literature? Is it reflected in your volunteer work with a particular group or cause such as unwed mothers, inmates, animal rescue, poverty, or illiteracy? Does it express itself in some form of instruction: an aerobics class, bilingual lessons, self-defense course, or recovery program? Is it best fulfilled through a contribution you'd like to make to society in education or politics? Or is it tied in with your lifestyle, with your personal longing to be married, to travel, or to live in the city?

Regardless of what your passion is, God gave you the gift of passion and made you his steward of it. So I have a question for you: why not go ahead and live with the desires and purpose your Creator intended? God wants to use every part of you, including the passions he chose for you and stirs within you. He wants your passion to be alive and well and available to him whenever he wants to use it for his purposes. Perhaps now is the time to take the step that will replace drudgery and apathy with an unquenchable zest for life.

This is the first step we've taken on the pathway to purpose that can compare to soaring on wings like eagles.[3] It is the opportunity of a lifetime to dance, laugh, play, and experiment with what makes your pulse race. When you fully embrace this step and understand that God has placed good desires in your heart, it can wipe away indecision and fear about unintentionally embarking on a mission that is not God-ordained. It answers the nagging questions like: *Why would God allow me, a serious sinner, to do what I love doing? What if God doesn't approve of my deepest desires? What if I'm supposed to be doing something I dislike rather than this fun assignment?*

But even more important, taking this step will stir up your hunger for God. As you evaluate the desires of your heart, you will recognize God as your heart's most passionate desire. You will fall in love with him more deeply. When you

> *Success*
> *[Read: Passion!]*
> *is waking up in the morning, whoever you are, wherever you are, however old or young, and bounding out of bed because there's something out there that you love to do, that you believe in, that you're good at— something that's bigger than you are and you can hardly wait to go at it again today. It is something you'd rather be doing than anything else. You wouldn't give it up for more money, because it means more to you than money.*[4]
> WHIT HOBBS

understand that God, who knit you together in your mother's womb, also placed his desires for you in your heart, it will remind you of his magnificent investment in you. That alone will cause you to worship him, thank him, and desire him and his purposes all the more.

Living according to the desires of your heart won't take away all your trials, obstacles, and challenges. What God's gift of passion will do for you, though, is set you free to live without the guilt or uncertainty about what you should or should not do to please God. If you simply do what he designed you to do and be, you will find significance beyond measure. You will have a dream to work toward, a destiny to fulfill, a God to serve, a grand symphony to attend. So enjoy his gift of passion and let the music begin!

PASSION THAT SIZZLES

God has been harnessing the passions of women to accomplish his purposes for thousands of years. Miriam was passionate about singing,[5] Dorcas about sewing,[6] and Anna about praying and fasting.[7] Then there was Ruth, a widow who was passionate about family.[8] She remarried and went on to become the great grandmother of King David and an ancestor of Jesus! Who but God could use the desires of a woman's heart so effectively for his service? We can be grateful that he is still doing that for women today.

Some women friends of mine have dedicated their passions to God for his use. One woman coordinates a "MCs for JC" motorcycle ministry. A corporate HR director, she bonds easily with all kinds of people, cherishes relationships, and cares deeply about the stories of those she meets. She and her husband share a love of motorcycles and the great outdoors. It all comes together when she is able to talk with bikers about Jesus.

Another woman loves the people of Asia and leads evangelistic mission trips to China. One is passionate about justice and volunteers at a women's abuse shelter. One plays the piano to worship God and to inspire her Bible teaching. Another does needlepoint with the elderly while she tells them stories about Jesus. Yet another has a long-term dream of restoring a Victorian house to use as a retreat center for pastors and their spouses.

And here is one of my favorites. Julia is passionate about snowboarding and working with girls' youth ministries. When she is invited to speak at a retreat for teenage girls at a ski resort, she realizes anew how deeply passionate God is about the spiritual growth of youth. Her heart skips a beat when hanging out and sharing fun times lead to potentially life-changing conversations. Who but God could have imagined a ministry of snowboard-discipleship? Only he could orchestrate something that remarkable.

These women have felt the thrill of God in their triumphs, yet have deflected the honor to him. They have rejoiced in his love and direction. They have surrendered their strengths and hopes to their heavenly Father to do with as he wishes. They have faced adversity, have risked all, and have given 110 percent to their passionate dreams.

Where has your passion shown up through the varied seasons of your life? As a child, were you passionate about raising an animal, reading detective stories, or drawing? As a teen or young adult, were you passionate about environmental issues, playing volleyball, or getting straight A's in high school? As an adult, have you been passionate about having a child, building Habitat for Humanity houses, or teaching English as a second language? What have you done with those passions? God gave them to you for a purpose—to be used for his glory and his plans. Will you join him in that purpose?

WHAT? NO PASSION?

It is possible that our exploration of God-given passion has been unsettling to you. It may sound like a great idea, but you may be thinking, *I had passion once upon a time, but I sure can't find it now. What does God want me to do about that?*

First of all, don't fret. All of us go through dry spells and tough seasons of life when our passions take a back burner. Terri, for example, derives extraordinary delight from taking black-and-white photographs of unusual people, places, and things. When she has a camera in her hand, she always says, "Life doesn't get any better than this!" But recently she had to make some hard choices about how photography fits with her family's needs, her church ministry, and her career. Being a fanatic about taking pictures was causing conflicts with her top-priority commitments. Life circumstances have forced her to shift her attention away from photography for a while, but it will likely resurface when things settle down for her.

God who created you and watches over you sees all that is happening in your life. He knows your obligations and commitments and why you may have put your passions on temporary hold. But he knows more than that. He knows when fear, guilt, shattered dreams, fatigue, a broken heart, or heavy responsibilities may be hiding the desires of your heart from view. He knows if you are so overwhelmed that you can't seem to *go there* in your mind. If this is your situation, ask God to use his intimate knowledge of you to draw you closer to him, to heal you, to strengthen you, and/or to help you trust him more. Ask him to take you—when the timing is right—from the dispassionate place you are right now to a passionate place that holds great joy for you.

WHEN PASSION FIZZLES

One of my clients, Debbie, woke up one morning and no longer wanted to go boating and water-skiing. The lack of interest surprised her because those activities were her passion, something she had done eagerly every other weekend for the previous two summers. She tried to have fun on subsequent outings, but she felt no pizzazz. For her, the thrill of water sports had evaporated.

Why the sudden change? It might have been because Debbie's need for that java-type jolt had been met. Recently she had turned thirty-one, so perhaps she had mellowed and moved on. But after several meetings, Debbie and I uncovered a more complex reason for her sudden lack of passion.

Debbie had loved water sports because it felt so good to excel at something. She was proud of her accomplishments and enjoyed being admired by her friends. The personal reward she received from her passion was so satisfying that she never thought to look beyond the thrill. She never tried to anchor her passion to the rest of her life by considering how it applied to her daily roles or God's vision for her life. She clung to her passion strictly for her own pleasure and missed out on the added privilege of using her passion to further God's work.

It really isn't surprising that Debbie's passion died. The fire was doomed to go out because she wasn't connecting her passion with her basic, heaven-sent life purposes. Her passion for water sports never became part of following God wholeheartedly, like the Bible teaches.[9] As Debbie's passion quickly faded, she wondered why she was experiencing apathy, emptiness, and boredom. She asked me: "Is waterskiing all there is to life?" and "What am I supposed to do with myself now?"

How Will You Fill the Passion Void?

The questions Debbie was asking reveal just how essential passion is to our lives. Without God-ordained passion in our lives, we are vulnerable to a number of unhealthy outcomes. In his writings, Dr. Viktor Frankl describes the boredom and emptiness of a passionless life as an "existential vacuum." He identifies a specific related condition he calls "Sunday neurosis," which is a type of depression that sets in when the busy rush of the work week is over and people feel within themselves the true emptiness of their lives. He goes on to expose some of the inherent dangers facing people without passionate purpose:

> They are haunted by the experience of their inner emptiness, a void within themselves. . . . Not a few cases of suicide can be traced back to this existential vacuum. Such widespread phenomena as depression,

aggression, and addiction are not understandable unless we recognize the existential vacuum underlying them.[10]

A lack of passion can quickly turn into a serious problem, especially if we attempt to fill that void with unhealthy passions. There is no denying the compelling, attractive force of passions for gambling, alcohol, pornography, overspending, overeating, adultery, or drugs. Even innocent-sounding intoxicators like television talk shows all day long, constant shopping, perpetual telephone conversations, or obsessive-compulsive housecleaning can be destructive ways of feeding an unmet need for real passion. If we want to truly experience the desires of our heart and discover God's purpose, we must guard against the seductive power of these unhealthy passions.

When it comes to dealing with unhealthy passions, we need to be aware and exercise discernment. Sometimes they can represent a need to dull emotional pain or escape. Other times they have to do with a need for control, instant gratification, recklessness, or putting self first. Often, they are based on a sense of entitlement, an attitude of *I earned it. I deserve it.* Most often, they simply are an attempt to fill a void that can only be filled by Jesus and the meaning and purpose he brings to life.

So, if you struggle in this area, let healthy, God-given passions help protect you against unhealthy passions. Tell God you want the Spirit-filled passions he instilled in you, not the harmful ones you could import. By shifting your focus, you'll be busy for a lifetime. You won't even have time to seek out unhealthy outlets!

Whether you are in a passion-filled or passion-deprived time of your life, always remember to measure your passion choices against your value system, family dynamics, and Christian beliefs. By prayer and self-examination you will know if your passions are in line with your God-given priorities.

> *Women are more aware of what's on their gravestone, which is not, "I worked for IBM."*[11]
> FORMER LABOR SECRETARY LYNN MARTIN

LOOK FORWARD TO WHAT GOD WILL DO

God knows that the best ministries in life often involve several areas of a woman's passion. For example, my top five passions are that I have a huge heart for women, I love Sherlock Holmes mysteries, I can't get enough of jigsaw puzzles, I crave life purpose, and I am a travel enthusiast. So, what perfect purpose did God graciously orchestrate for me out of the sheer goodness of his heart? I help women put the mysterious puzzles of their lives together by encouraging them to reflect on their current and long-term purposes. And, as a speaker and missionary to women around the world, I travel.

Only God could have designed such a perfect fulfillment of my passions. Do you now see how important it is to identify the desires of your heart and allow them to become part of your daily life? Don't wait a lifetime to get started, like I nearly did, before you invite God to unveil his purpose-filled passions in your life. Take the step today. You'll be so glad you did!

THE SOJOURNER'S GUIDE TO DELIGHTING IN YOUR PASSIONS

The following suggestions are designed to help you find and nurture the God-given desires of your heart. Start today, but be careful not to rush the process. Take as much time as you need to uncover your passions and discover how they flow into God's purpose for your life.

Some Basic Hints to Get Started

To get a clear picture of the desires of your heart, try out several of the following ideas that have proven helpful to women over the years:

- Hang around passionate people. Expect some of their energy to rub off on you!

✥ Ask family and friends what they've noticed about your desires or potential passions.

✥ Write some brief entries in your spiritual journal about your times of greatest joy, regardless of their size, scope, or nature. Ask God to reveal any desires and passions that might be related to those times of joy.

✥ Get out of your rut! Do something different, unusual, out of your normal routine. Go ahead—burn your expensive candles and use your guest towels, volunteer at your local animal shelter, try out that new Moroccan restaurant, join a book discussion group, sign up for a recreational sports league, or spend time visiting at a nursing home or hospital. Do whatever is needed to get you out of your humdrum box and inspire you to think beyond your daily grind.

✥ Once you recognize several of your passions, dedicate them to God—and enjoy them.

Guard Against Jealousy

Guard against jealousy of other people's desires, dreams, and passionate assignments from God. Fight diligently against envy: track it, expose it, hate it, renounce it, and flee from it. One of the best ways I have found to do this is to help others fulfill their exciting dreams. Pray for them, encourage them, assist them, introduce them to people who can cheer them on, share your resources with them, and coach them.

Daydream

Whether or not you are ready for a new career or ministry today, spend some time thinking about one that would ignite your passion. Daydream about it as if the sky's the limit. This exercise will give you an out-of-the-box perspective. Ask God to show you a desire or passion that you could begin to investigate when the time is right.

Go for It!

Experiment. Follow your hunches until you feel passionate about something that's legal, moral, and ethical! Let the process take as long as it needs to take. Don't rush the discovery.

You may want to work as a volunteer in a library, become a soccer coach, or teach a Sunday school class. Feel free to blame me if someone asks why you suddenly are learning to decorate cakes, folk dance, scuba dive, or fly planes. Try out your ideas with low-cost probes, one by one. But don't send me the bill!

Be sure to pursue other desires of your heart such as adoption, career change, relocation, or travel. Consider also major contributions to society that connect with your heart's desires such as putting prayer back in school, helping prostitutes get off the streets, or starting a Christian talk show. One more bit of advice: if you have a growing passion for any big ideas, pace yourself!

RECOMMENDED BOOKS ON PASSION

What Color Is Your Parachute? by Richard Bolles[12]
The Power of Uniqueness, by Arthur Miller Jr. and Bill Hendricks[13]

NOW IS THE TIME TO LIVE PASSIONATELY

Will you take this next step toward God and his purpose for your life: *to expect God to give you the desires of your heart?* Do you feel grateful for God's gift of passion to you? Do you understand how living passionately draws you closer to him, how it bonds your heart to his heart?

If you have found your passion and harnessed its energy, then watch the spectacular fireworks as God shows you how to honor your family, church, neighborhood, and world with his gift. He wants to use every part of you, including your aching desire to accomplish his work on earth. If you are just beginning to discover your passion, ask God to fan the flames. If your passion has waned, ask God to give you spiritual CPR today to revive it!

GOD'S WISDOM FOR THE PATHWAY

THE "HANNAH" STEP OF LIFE: EXPECT GOD TO GIVE YOU THE DESIRES OF YOUR HEART

For a lesson from Hannah during this step of your life, read 1 Samuel 1:1–2:11. Hannah so passionately wanted a son that she tearfully poured her heart out to the Lord in prayer, saying that if God blessed her with a son, she would dedicate him to the Lord's service. Eli, a priest who was watching Hannah pray, said to her: "Go in peace, and may the God of Israel grant you what you have asked of him" (1:17). Later, Hannah conceived Samuel. After he was weaned, she took him to the temple to live. Are you as passionate about something as Hannah was? Will you surrender your passion to the Lord to do with as he chooses?

Personal Pathway Questions

Look at your passions in several categories: as a hobby you love, a personal longing you have, a group or cause you want to help, or a contribution you'd love to make. This simple mechanism will help you think of answers to the question, "What are you passionate about?" from four different perspectives.

1. What *hobby* are you passionate about?
   - Baseball
   - Collecting antiques
   - Fishing
   - Gourmet cooking
   - Mountain climbing
   - Quilting
   - Reading
   - Snorkeling

2. What personal *longing or hope* are you passionate about?
   - Country house with a white picket fence
   - Financial security
   - Having children
   - Marriage
   - Private counseling practice
   - Screenplay contract
   - Travel

3. What *group or cause* do you have a passionate ache for in your heart?
   - Elderly
   - Endangered species
   - Illiterate
   - Immigrants
   - Justice
   - Pro-life
   - Rain forests
   - Unemployed

4. What passionate *contribution* do you dream about making?
   - Becoming a short-term missionary
   - Evangelizing movie producers
   - Feeding the homeless
   - Lobbying for handicap rights
   - Starting a choir

5. Looking back over your answers to Questions 1–4, in what way might God purposefully use one or more of your passions to give you a unique kingdom-building assignment? There are no wrong answers. Let your creativity take over.

NOTES

1. (p. 150) James 1:14 warns, "But each one is tempted when, by his own evil desire, he is dragged away and enticed."
2. (p. 151) Bob Buford, *Halftime: Changing Your Game Plan from Success to Significance* (Grand Rapids: Zondervan, 1994), 81.
3. (p. 152) See Isaiah 40:31.
4. (p. 152) Whit Hobbs, *I LOVE ADVERTISING* (New York: Adweek Books, 1985), 14–15.
5. (p. 153) See Exodus 15:20–21.
6. (p. 153) See Acts 9:39–40.
7. (p. 153) See Luke 2:36–37.
8. (p. 153) See Ruth 1:16–18.
9. (p. 156) See Joshua 14:6–15, especially verse 8.
10. (p. 157) Viktor Frankl, *Man's Search for Meaning* (Boston: Beacon Press), 111–112. 1959, 1962, 1984, 1992 by Viktor Frankl. Reprinted by permission of Beacon Press.
11. (p. 157) Quoted in Betty Morris and Ruth Coxeter, "Executive Women Confront Mid-life Crisis," *Fortune*, 18 September 1995.
12. (p. 160) Richard Bolles, *What Color Is Your Parachute?* (Berkeley, Calif.: Ten Speed Press, 1995, updated annually).
13. (p. 160) Arthur Miller Jr. and Bill Hendricks, *The Power of Uniqueness* (Grand Rapids: Zondervan, 2002).

Chapter 10

SURRENDER YOUR DAILY LIFE TO GOD

*Take your everyday, ordinary life—your sleeping, eating, going-to-work,
and walking-around life—and place it before God as an offering.*
(ROMANS 12:1, MSG)

If by this point on the journey you think you're ready for long, leaping strides toward purpose, our next step may surprise or even disappoint you. You see, the stepping-stone, *surrender your everyday, ordinary life to God as an offering*, isn't one step at all; it is a closely clustered group of small stepping-stones. At first glance, this step baffles many women. I've watched them stand immobile before this cluster of stones and stare in bewilderment. They look at the stones, they look at me, they look at the stones again. Sometimes they ask aloud, "Is this really the way? The stones are so small and so many. How will they ever lead me toward my big purpose?"

Trust me, they will. The process of taking many incremental steps of surrender actually makes it easier to carefully consider each decision you make to offer your life to God. Furthermore, the size of the stepping-stone is not a true indicator of how difficult the step will be or how far it will take you. But, once taken, even the smallest steps of obedience will cause you to develop quickly in your faith.

Some women, however, balk at the idea of surrender. They want to do something meaningful for God, but they want to control what it is, when they do it, and how it will be done. Surrender has no place in their plans. Other women simply can't believe that God actually expects them to completely surrender every aspect of their lives to him. And, because the Holy Spirit never coerces anyone to surrender, these women stand frozen in place. Years fly by as they continue to pass up the steps of opportunity that God has placed before them.

So what about you? Do you want to take the next step in knowing God and his purposes for your life? Have you grown so close to him by walking the pathway to purpose that you are willing to take any step he wants you to take? Then let's find out what this series of stepping-stones is all about.

WHY IS SURRENDER SO IMPORTANT?

We simply cannot fulfill God's greatest purpose for us without surrendering our will and life to him. Surrender, which can be defined as "the act of giving up one's person or possessions into the authority of another . . . of relinquishing one's power, aims, or goals,"[1] is a thoughtful, intentional, daily response to the Holy Spirit. It is coming into agreement with him that Christ is our King and that we will serve him above all else. It begins the moment we agree to make Jesus Christ our Savior and Lord and continues as we increasingly grant him lordship over all areas of life including our family, ministry, finances, home, job, hobbies, relationships, education, emotions, spiritual growth, and more.

Surrender is essential to our *sanctification*, which is the never-ending process by which we are freed from sin and set apart for God's work and purposes. Surrender is about learning to live for an audience of one, and that is God. It involves our minute-by-minute turning away from all the idols in life. It means we let go of everything that takes a higher priority than God—whatever we hold tightly—whether that is success, travel, talents, compulsions, relationships, or any other life-priority idol.

If the Lord is calling you to turn something over to him, I urge you to respond. Whether your surrender takes years, months, or a moment; whether you release something physical, spiritual, or emotional, I urge you to start taking the small steps of surrender that God has placed in your path. When you do, your eyes will be opened to truths that lead you to surrender even more control to God.

> *Evidence of a surrendered life is always obedience.*[2]
> RICK WARREN

If you happen to be a woman who is a tad bit controlling and inclined to resist this step, you may want to ready yourself to face the honest truth. Perhaps it is time to remember that all of creation belongs to God. Our lives are simply on loan to us. God has every right to command our surrender, and someday he will do just that! The Bible tells us that even "the mighty deep" will one day announce "its surrender to the Lord."[3] So the only question is whether we bow to God now or later.

God gave you free will, his permission for you to choose how you will live while you are on this earth, and he will not infringe upon it. He will not demand that you surrender at this time. He will not browbeat you into it nor beg you for it. Instead, he will wait patiently until you voluntarily surrender your life as a precious offering to him.

Following God is no hobby. As surrendered women, our foremost question is not, "What do I want?" or even "What do I want to do for God?" Rather, the question of a surrendered heart that desires God's purposes above all else is, "What does the God of the universe want *for* me and *from* me?"

So How Do We "Do" Surrender?

Once we've fought the "my way, your way" battle with God and agreed that surrender will be our way of life, how do we do it? When do we know we are supposed to surrender something? How do we know what we are supposed to surrender?

Great questions! God provides surrender opportunities in many different ways, so we have to learn to recognize them. The Holy Spirit will always, in some way, prompt you to surrender and give you the opportunity to decide how to respond. He may nudge you through an impression, a Scripture passage, a friend's comment, an incident, a season of grief, or dozens of other means. He may reveal his message through a persistent thought, perhaps one that occurs to you several times during the day or the first thing when you wake up in the morning. Don't be surprised if a prompting for surrender even comes out of the blue while you are waiting in a slow-moving, drive-through line at a fast food restaurant!

What kinds of surrender opportunities does God give us? Well, God may ask you to turn over control of your goals and future plans. He may ask you to trust him with your fears, longings, or relationships. He may ask you to give him things as diverse as your addiction to sweets, your desire to be popular, your escalating credit card debt, your old life scripts, or your most favored possessions.

Be forewarned that an affirmative response to the Holy Spirit in one area (whether minor or major) will have a snowball effect, prompting you to surrender to God territory you had previously declared "off-limits" to him. This happens because every little step of surrender causes your heart to soften toward the heart of God. Every step of surrender enlarges your vision to see his perspective more clearly.

Be aware, too, that you will be making some extremely difficult choices during this step, so please be patient with yourself. I repeat: please be patient with yourself! Don't spend one moment fretting or being upset with yourself because you're not perfect—not one of us is. But God *is* perfect, and as we surrender we can count on him to love us in our imperfection and draw us ever closer to himself and his purposes.

Surrender is one of the greatest challenges of faith you will face, but step by step God will prepare you to be completely his, to be totally engaged in his purposes for your life. As you walk with God more closely every day, you will be increasing your trust in the Lord of lords, and Jesus will become totally sufficient for you. Eventually the day will come, if it has not already, when the Holy Spirit taps you on the shoulder and asks, "Will you now give your entire life to Christ? Will you submit to the plan the Lord lovingly crafted for you?" What a humbling privilege it is to be asked to give your all for Christ right in the midst of your life circumstances.

STUBBORN ME

It is painful for me to admit it, but I have been one of the Holy Spirit's most stubborn cases when it comes to surrender. I have dodged surrender in every way possible. I've tried to ignore the steps of surrender. I've pretended they were too small to bother with, and at other times I've convinced myself they were too big to attempt. I've resisted God in regard to surrendering my tithe, career, life dreams, this book, and my *wants versus needs* mentality. None of these, however, compares to the lengthy battles I have fought regarding my surrender of nicotine, my home, my children, and sugar.

Surrendering Nicotine

I began smoking when I was a teenager and continued for seventeen years. Eventually I became concerned enough about the health implications of my addiction that I attempted to quit. For four years I tried everything humanly possible, but nothing worked. I ripped up cigarettes. I flushed them down toilets. I crushed them with the heel of my shoe. I even refused to purchase them, which led to "Can I bum a cigarette?" What a joke!

I managed to quit smoking the moment I found out I was pregnant with my first child, but I picked up the habit again after he was born. (Forgive me. We didn't know about secondhand smoke back then.) That's about the time my husband and I got serious about attending church regularly. After a particularly convicting Sunday sermon about godly lifestyle changes, I knew smoking was something I needed to give up to God. Due to my past failures to quit, I thought it was absolutely impossible, but I halfheartedly asked God to help me stop smoking anyway.

I have no doubt that it was God who then instituted a "No Smoking" policy in my life. The very next day, he arranged for me to have an experience I'll never forget. On Monday morning I was swimming laps in our community's indoor pool. As I caught my breath at the end of some laps, I grew more and more nauseated by the sickeningly sweet smell of cigarettes on the hair, skin, and breath of the chatty man in the lane next to me. His overpowering aroma permeated the fog hovering above the surface of the heated water. I have not had a cigarette since that day when God placed me in what I call his Personalized Anti-Smoking Treatment Center. Today I can't even look at someone puffing on a cigarette (even through rolled up car windows) without having a near-gag reaction.

Before I surrendered my nicotine habit to God, I never could have imagined the spiritual impact that quitting smoking would have on me. I learned that God was powerful enough to help me deal with things that I was powerless to handle. That knowledge makes it easier now for me to surrender to him in other areas. It makes it easier for me to trust him to handle all of my weaknesses. If God could help me quit smoking, I know he can do anything!

Surrendering My Home and Children

Probably the hardest thing for me to surrender to God—and this may sound silly because you may be expecting me to say *my children*— was the huge, five-bedroom home I purchased five years after my divorce. I knew that my home belonged to God and that I was simply a steward of what he had entrusted to me, but that didn't keep it from becoming an idol. My wonderful house in its expensive zip code supplied status. I couldn't imagine giving it up, especially if God wanted me to live somewhere I didn't like.

I eventually realized I was supposed to sell that house, but for a full year I dug in my heels and refused to do it. What a nightmare I lived trying to untangle God's best for my life while still continuing to weave in my stubborn wishes. But God was persistent. He kept reminding me of his desire through the wise counsel of my brother Paul and sister Cathy. He continued to impress on me the need to downsize and simplify my life.

> *Many are the plans in a [woman's] heart, but it is the LORD'S purpose that prevails.*
> (PROVERBS 19:21)

I finally came to the point where I knew I simply needed to obey God and sell the house. When I moved into a smaller home, I suddenly had much more time and energy. I found that I could focus more earnestly on my writing, which was something I had not been able to do previously with all the repairs, chores, and decorating.

As terrible as it sounds, it was easier for me to surrender my children to God than it was to trust him with my home. Sad, huh? But I knew in my heart that my children would be in better hands with God than with me. While it was still excruciatingly hard to turn my children's lives over to him, I released them to his loving care by saying a simple, heartfelt prayer to that effect. Actually, I had to say that prayer many times. It seemed to take me forever to be able to voice words that were not a lie. Though I did not drop off my kids at the local temple to be raised by a holy man, like Hannah did with her son Samuel, I did choose to trust that God would love them and guide their lives better than I could.

Surrendering Sugar

I have spent my life chasing chocolate and idolizing ice cream. I've faithfully tried each of these brilliant plans to stop consuming it:

no sugar in the house

no sugar at the church office

no sugar without eating protein or a salad

no sugar while watching television

no sugar if I have to buy it

no sugar past 3 p.m. (except when it is offered as an official dinner dessert)

only two scoops of ice cream with no cone

only three scoops with no toppings

sugar on Sundays only

sugar only if it is a celebration (birthdays, weddings, graduations)

sugar only if it is a holiday (Halloween, Thanksgiving, Christmas, New Year's, Valentine's Day, Mother's Day, and on and on and on!)

Years ago, I got tired of living in that scrutinizing way, so I went on a one-year sugar fast. It was surprisingly easy, but my sugar intake became extreme again as soon as the fast ended. I've been on and off sugar for four years now because I'm still unable to enjoy it in moderation.

My on-again, off-again surrender of sugar has taught me, among other things, that God loves it when I fast from sugar just to honor him. Whenever we choose to honor God by giving up something that has become an idol in our lives, he honors our action. I have found that I learn more about prayer, purpose, preparation, or some other aspect of spiritual growth whenever I surrender an idol to him. So I will continue to ask him to teach me through this process.

GOD'S RICH REWARDS FOR SURRENDER

Learning to surrender is more than a warm-up drill that readies us heart and soul for a future, "Big Kahuna" purpose in life. Bowing to the lordship of Christ is also a distinct, tangible purpose for today that begins paying compound dividends immediately. Consider for a moment the life-changing rewards God showers upon us when we surrender to Christ our King.

We give an offering to God when we surrender, but he gives us far more in return. As we surrender to God, he begins to transform our lives. The result of a transformed life is that we experience the precious blessings of his Spirit: "love, joy, peace, patience, kindness, goodness, faithfulness, gentleness and self-control."[4] The more we surrender, the more we are transformed, and the more these blessings flow from the Spirit to us. I can't think of a more valuable commodity on the market today than these nine Holy Spirit-filled outcomes of surrender. If you and I could bottle these things and sell them, we'd be very rich women. Yet God gives them in abundance to women who surrender to him and serve him with their lives.

In addition, consider the thank-you bonus that comes when you surrender your day-to-day comings and goings, your problems, and your concerns to the Magnificent Counselor. He will give you all the wisdom and focus needed to live a life of worship, gratitude, service, and purpose. By teaming up with the one who can prepare you for upcoming dangers and opportunities, you will become more receptive to godly insight about how to manage your roles and navigate your choices. Think of all the downtime, prayer time, family time, and ministry time you'll have as a result. What a relief! What an excellent return on your surrender investment.

Yet God gives you an even more valuable reward for your surrender. When you humbly give up your way and do whatever he asks of you, big or small, you please the God of the universe who promises never to desert you. What a payoff! But think about it for a minute. Is it enough? Is surrender really worth it?

THE LONGEST STEP OF ALL

During a message that Kay Warren, my pastor's wife, gave at a church conference, she raised a tough question related to surrender. She asked a group of us if we would still follow God even if he never did another thing for us.[5] As a woman who has struggled with surrender and has also seen the rich rewards of it, I needed to give that question some thought. *What if God didn't help me with my big dream of making a difference in the world?* I wondered. *Would I still follow him?*

My thoughts caused me to wonder if I would even *love* God, let alone *follow* him, if I lost everything—my children included. Would I love him if I became terminally ill? I'm not proud to say it, but my initial answers to those questions were absolutely self-centered. Here is verbatim what I wrote in my spiritual journal: "Quite honestly, I would go through the necessary Christian motions, but I would be mad at God—real mad."

Of course I knew what the correct answer should have been and what I wanted it to be, but I couldn't honestly make it my own for several days. I had to do what I call my "processing thing" with the information, and that is never a pretty sight. I tend to proceed dramatically through all of Elisabeth Kübler-Ross's five stages of grief: denial, anger, bargaining, depression, and (after much wailing!), acceptance. Finally, I could pray as sincerely as I knew how at the time:

> God, today, I empty myself to be filled by you. Give me the grace to love you whether or not you bless my family or me anymore. I am content with whatever you choose to bless me with—or even subtract from me—my kids, eyes, hands, voice, limbs, energy, or possessions. They are all yours, not mine. I am sorry for my arrogance in acting as though I was giving something to you that belonged to me. In reality, everything I have is already yours; it's simply on loan to me. I leave everything in your hands. You have big hands. I trust you.

I have continued to pray that prayer since that time. I have also found and grown to love a Bible passage that speaks of surrender to God no matter what:

> Though the fig tree does not bud
> and there are no grapes on the vines,
> though the olive crop fails
> and the fields produce no food,
> though there are no sheep in the pen

and no cattle in the stalls,
yet I will rejoice in the LORD.
I will be joyful in God my Savior.
The Sovereign LORD is my strength;
he makes my feet like the feet of a deer,
he enables me to go on the heights.[6]

The writer of that passage, Habakkuk, makes it clear that he would rejoice in God in spite of the hardship God would allow to come to the people of Judah. Habakkuk took a step of surrender and chose to follow God even though nothing good was in clear sight. We too have a similar choice. Will you take a step of surrender? Will you choose to follow God even if he never does another thing for you?

THE SOJOURNER'S GUIDE TO STEP-BY-STEP SURRENDER

The following action steps for surrender will help you discover areas of your life God wants you to surrender to him. Practice these action steps for the next ten days to establish some new habits that will help you move forward on the pathway to purpose.

The Ten-Day Challenge

Revelation—Seek the Truth

Initially, do nothing but be still and quiet your soul. Ask the Holy Spirit to show up during this ten-day process to reveal the truth to you about any relationship, situation, possession, feeling, or activity that may be blocking you from fulfilling your purposes on earth. Listen intently. Saturate this time in prayer and Bible reading. Expect the Holy Spirit to give you an impression regarding a person, place, thing, emotion, or behavior you may be holding too tightly.

Investigation—Do Your Footwork and Homework

To help you make your final decision about surrendering what the Holy Spirit would like you to surrender, think and act like an investigator in search of truth. Make a phone call, read a book, talk with a

Christian counselor, and/or attend an appropriate conference. Keep asking questions and pursuing answers until you come to a conclusion about your next step of surrender.

Calculation—Count the Cost

Evaluate what might change if God decides to take what you have surrendered. The Bible warns us to count the cost: "So no one can become my disciple unless [she] first sits down and counts [her] blessings—and then renounces them all for me."[7] Ask yourself: "What if God takes my car, parents, savings account, small group, company profits, personal comfort, time, or health?" Prepare yourself to actually *let go* of what you say you are surrendering. Guard against bargaining tactics such as, "God, I'll surrender this to you if you will. . . ." This isn't a hostage negotiation where you get to demand what you want to receive in return for what you are about to surrender. God owns everything already! Your options are "A": Surrender, or "B": Don't surrender.

Transformation—Think with the Mind of Christ

After the Holy Spirit has revealed a surrender opportunity to you and you have done your homework and counted the cost, follow the advice of the apostle Paul and deliberately apply the mind of Christ to your upcoming response: "Do not conform any longer to the pattern of this world, but be transformed by the renewing of your mind. Then you will be able to test and approve what God's will is—his good, pleasing and perfect will."[8]

Set your sights on becoming more like Christ. Focus on him and ask him to transform your thinking. Study appropriate Scripture passages as you surrender a particular area of your life. If you desire anything less than permanent transformation, you are not considering surrender; you are considering nothing more than a New Year's resolution that is waiting to be broken.

Declaration—Publicly Give Up Control of Your Will

Tell God you are willing to throw away one ugly idol. Because surrender is an act of your will, not a function of your emotion or feeling, write an official declaration of your chosen course of action. You can write your declaration in a journal, even if you have to write it in secret code as I have done many times to throw unauthorized readers off my trail. Then, state your decision to another Christian and ask that person to hold you accountable.

Dedication—Prayerfully Begin

Surround yourself with one or more prayer warriors who will commit to praying for you to actually do the surrendering! Ask them to pray for as long as it takes. Then watch for a radical response or rescue from our amazing God, even if his acknowledgment takes longer than you expect.

The One-Day Challenge

If all of this seems too hard for you right now, take a "One-Day Surrender Challenge." Prayerfully and purposefully choose to surrender one thing that has a hold over you (anything from coffee to television to the telephone!) for twenty-four hours. Watch for and record any blessings that result in your relationships, energy level, or other areas, such as your attitude.

RECOMMENDED BOOKS ON SALVATION AND SURRENDER

The Case for Christ, by Lee Strobel[9]
The Sacred Romance, by Brent Curtis and John Eldredge[10]

Now Is the Time to Surrender All

Will you take this next step toward God and his purpose for your life and *surrender your everyday, ordinary life to God as an offering?* If you don't surrender control of your life to Jesus Christ, you will surrender—by default—to hopelessness. How can I say that so emphatically? Because when it comes to surrender we serve either God or the Devil.

A life that is a living sacrifice to God is a magnificent and powerful thing. I pray that you will heed the advice of Romans 12 about offering yourself as a living sacrifice, holy and pleasing to God as "your spiritual act of worship."[11] Throughout my childhood, I had the privilege of seeing my parents surrender every possession and every aspect of their lives to God. No matter what the consequences of turning something over to his control, no matter how impossible the circumstances appeared, they surrendered to God and trusted him to care for them. Their faith, their surrender, was truly an act of worship.

When my mother died in 1996, I had a vivid dream of her first day in heaven that I would like to share with you. She was bowing low to our Lord God, who was seated on a throne, high and exalted. The train of his robe filled the temple. My mom had her face buried in her arms, attempting to protect her eyes from the blinding light of God's presence. She was so humbly stunned by God's beauty and so completely surrendered to him that all she could do was whisper repeatedly, "Holy, holy, holy."[12]

May I offer a blessing for your ongoing surrender? I pray that you will be "an instrument for noble purposes, made holy, useful to the Master and prepared to do any good work."[13] May the rest of your life exhibit evidence of the surrendering you will do today and next week and next month.

GOD'S WISDOM FOR THE PATHWAY

THE "MARY, MOTHER OF JESUS" STEP OF LIFE: SURRENDERING YOUR EVERYDAY, ORDINARY LIFE TO GOD

For a lesson from Mary, the mother of Jesus, read Luke 1:26–38. Mary's life was turned upside down the day the angel appeared to her with the news that she would be the mother of the Savior of the world. When she said yes to the angel, she was agreeing to let the Holy Spirit use her for God's glory. Did you know that she could have been stoned to death for being pregnant out of wedlock? If God had asked you, instead of Mary, to surrender all your plans and dreams for a comfortable life and risk being stoned to death (or any other gruesome method of dying), what would you have said?

Ask yourself: "What am I refusing to surrender to God today?" and then pray about dedicating that to the Almighty.

Personal Pathway Questions

1. Describe one of your surrender journeys thus far with a particular person, place, thing, emotion, or issue. What has it taught you about God and yourself?

2. What is God nudging you to do about surrendering to him? (Is it to seek the truth; do your footwork and homework; count the cost; think with the mind of Christ; publicly give up control of your will; and/or prayerfully begin?) Why do you say that?

3. How would you complete this sentence and why? *I am ready to surrender both the good and bad parts of my life to God, including my* _____. (Consider your house, car, career, ministry, family, children, past, present, future, dreams, finances, addictions, fears, distractions, sins, hobbies, projects, fame, material

possessions, power, reputation, spiritual growth, community work, friends, dark secrets, education.)

Regardless of whether you surrendered anything today or not, you may want to say this prayer:

Lord, please take me from where I am today. You are acutely aware of how important _____ is/are to me. Help me to trust and obey you on a daily, hourly, and minute-by-minute basis.

NOTES

1. (p. 166) William Morris, ed., *The American Dictionary of the English Language* (Boston: Houghton Mifflin, 1981), 1295.
2. (p. 167) From "Path to Personal Peace," a sermon given 16 May, 1999, at Saddleback Church, Lake Forest, Calif. Used with permission.
3. (p. 167) Habakkuk 3:10, TLB.
4. (p. 173) Galatians 5:22–23.
5. (p. 173) Kay Warren, "How to Keep the Ministry From Killing You," an address given at a church growth conference in May 1997 at Saddleback Church, Lake Forest, Calif. Used with permission.
6. (p. 175) Habakkuk 3:17–19.
7. (p. 176) Luke 14:33, TLB.
8. (p. 176) Romans 12:2.
9. (p. 177) Lee Strobel, *The Case for Christ* (Grand Rapids: Zondervan, 1998).
10. (p. 177) Brent Curtis and John Eldredge, *The Sacred Romance*, text and workbook (Nashville: Thomas Nelson, 1997).
11. (p. 178) Romans 12:1.
12. (p. 178) See Isaiah 6:1–3.
13. (p. 178) 2 Timothy 2:21.

Part Six

Point Others *toward* *the* Pathway

God's *Evangelism* Purpose for You:
To Complete His Mission for Your Life

Chapter 11

ANTICIPATE GOD'S VISION

He who forms the mountains, creates the wind, and reveals
his thoughts to man, he who turns dawn to darkness, and treads
the high places of the earth—the LORD God Almighty is his name.
(AMOS 4:13)

It seems like I have waited forever to share this next step with you. So I guess it won't matter if I wait a few more minutes, so that we can quickly recap how far we've come since our last backward glance in chapter five. Up to that point, we had forgotten the past, pressed on, focused on today, and loved others. Since then we have pursued peace, repented, washed some feet, became integrous, expected the desires of our hearts, and surrendered. Wow! I think we deserve a medal for making it this far!

But remember that infamous "Wall" in my marathon story from chapter one? We're there now. So let's throw some water on our faces, push each other along from behind, and then sprint to the finish line together. There will be plenty of time afterward to collapse on the grass and laugh out loud with joy!

The next stepping-stone, *eagerly anticipate that the Lord God Almighty will reveal his vision to you*, is actually my favorite one along the pathway to purpose. I get excited about it because every woman has a unique, custom-made, broad-reach life purpose, and God wants to reveal his thoughts about it to her. It is nothing less than thrilling when a woman catches sight of God's vision and begins to intentionally live out her God-ordained life purpose.

It breaks my heart, but many women never step on or past this stepping-stone. They come so close to receiving a revelation from God about their purpose—*the* most far-reaching contribution he put them on earth to make that can have ripple effects on countless people—yet they choose to stop here. Even though God personally inscribes this stepping-stone with each of our names, some of us don't seem to be able to recognize it as our own. Perhaps, when it comes down to it, we may not really want to know the purpose God has in mind for us. Or, we may be afraid of what God's purpose will require of us.

Only a small number of women are brave enough to prepare them-selves to receive a vision, ask God to reveal it, admit when they have seen it, seek advice amidst the confusion, or complete the work after they have their instructions. Why? Because vision crosses the line from taking small steps of faithful obedience to taking quantum leaps of obedience—and, frankly, that can be frightening. So my goal is not only to prepare you to hear God's thoughts about this stepping-stone in general, but to help you be receptive to the revelation and fulfillment of his vision for you. Then, you can scramble up the bank of the stream to begin living out his purpose for your life.

God Will Reveal His Vision!

Do you recall the popular television- and movie series, *Mission Impossible*? The plot always revolved around secret agents who per-formed spectacular feats in their efforts to save the world. I love the recurring phrase that preceded each assignment: "Your mission, should you decide to accept it. . . ." Wouldn't it be great if God sent you a mes-sage in an audible voice via a tape recorder or telephone, "This is your mission for the rest of your life. You will honor me, should you choose to accept it"?

I want to reassure you that God may not speak to you in an audible voice, but he will communicate his message. That's the incredible news the prophet Amos proclaims when he says that God "reveals his thoughts." That's what Daniel was explaining to King Nebuchadnezzar when he said there is a God in heaven who reveals secrets.[1] Our God, the God of Amos and Daniel, wants you to trust him to reveal his thoughts about your purpose. He not only has a vision for you, but when the timing is perfect, he will reveal it. Just as he was clear with prophets like Samuel and Isaiah when he chose them to carry his messages,[2] he will be clear with you. So let's make sure we understand what kind of vision we can expect from God.

Vision is an awareness of how God wants to use you in a bold way to accomplish his purposes. It is sensing your God-breathed destiny and seeing the monumental, humanly impossible task God has in mind for you. It is catching a glimpse of his multidimensional life strategy for you—the type of person he wants you to become and what he wants you to do for him.

God's primary vision for your life is already clearly revealed in the Bible. Basically we are to love God, love our neighbor,[3] and go and make disciples.[4] This broadly cast vision is our anchor point for living a purposeful life. But God's vision does not end there. He also reveals to each of us his individual, specific assignment in relationship to that broader vision.

God's unique vision for you can be described as a desire that steals your heart—either immediately or eventually—and shouts to you, "This is your sacred commission, far beyond your everyday purposes in life." It is the exclusive, heart-engaging work God prearranged for you before you were born. It is how you, and you alone, will minister with excellence in the eyes of the Lord.

When you receive such a vision, you see an opportunity that so draws you to it that you can't stay away from it. It compels you to share your intentions with other people. It is so inspiring and demanding that it leads you to gather others around you and mobilize them by your example. People are hungry to follow someone with vision, so until God reveals his vision for their lives, you may want to enlist them in your army of God's people who can help you reach your God-given goal.

When you discern God's vision for your life, you may be utterly stunned because fulfilling it will require tremendous faith, hope, and love. Accepting God's vision and carrying out your life purpose is like signing a service contract to work only for him for the rest of your life, no matter how tough things get. And, believe me, they will get tough. God's purpose will cost you your life in the sense that you must choose to die to self and accept his plan. It will cost you your life, too, in that you will be spent and used up in service to God. It will stretch you to such an impossible degree that you will fail without him.

Yet once vision is unleashed, it is like electricity that brings light to dark places. It is your personalized way of leading people from emptiness to surrender to significance in Christ. How amazing it is to look forward to God's vision!

Eager for Vision?

When we eagerly anticipate that the Lord God Almighty will reveal his vision, we are taking a bold and hopeful step toward purpose. Just consider the impact of anticipating that God will reveal his thoughts to you.

God's revealed thoughts, his vision for your life purpose, will increase your faith because you will need to trust him to show you things farther out than you can currently see. It will inspire you when you attempt to turn your daydreaming and brainstorming into the beginnings of a strategic plan. It will give you clarity for decisions and add definition to your goals and objectives. It will embolden you when things get tough. And, vision will enable you to organize your new venture around God's priorities, which is the best time management process ever conceived.

God's most generous gift during this step, though, is that he, the King of all kings, cares enough about you to talk with you about who he is and how you can serve him on earth. What a privilege for a mere mortal to hear from God! Living intentionally during this step will invite God to speak to you more and more often about his best long-term plans for you.

But anticipating God's vision can also haunt you with troubling "What if?" questions. Do any of these sound familiar to you? *What if I am doing something wrong that is preventing God from speaking to me? What if God already revealed his vision to me, and I missed it? What if I heard God's thoughts, but I don't want to do what he told me to do?*

These are all valid concerns, and they can cause you to fret to the point of emotional paralysis. If these or similar questions are bogging you down, do yourself a huge favor and give yourself a fresh start. Put your past, with its doubts and failures, behind you, and consider today as the first day of the rest of your life to live for God. This will give you a new perspective when God offers you another chance to hear his best plans for you.

Your job during this step is not to worry about God's revelation of his vision; it is to honor your commitment to him by following his instructions to "listen carefully to Me"[5] and "incline your ear, and come to Me."[6] If you faithfully listen to God, he will ease your concerns, help you overcome your stubbornness, and guide you through any corrective action you need to take to ready yourself. He is with you right now, helping you absorb the practical applications in this book.

BEGGING FOR A VISION

I was so eager for a vision from God that for years I begged him for one. Countless times I asked my dearest friends—Dianne, Elaine, and Diana—if they had figured out God's purpose for their lives or had any insight into what they thought God wanted of me. I was so serious about life and desperate to grab a vision that I couldn't think of anything more

When "how" God
wants us to undertake
our vision is unclear,
we must pray and wait
patiently. These are
the times when he
is equipping us—
preparing us—with
all we will need
to successfully fulfill
the vision. It may be
his will to keep things
unclear for forty years,
as in the case of
Moses. Keep moving
with what you've
seen so far, while
praying for what you
still need to see.[7]
PATRICK MORLEY

pertinent to talk about. Although God certainly created friends for intense times of talking, listening, caring, soul-searching, and crying together, I was often so hungry for God's vision that I missed out on some of the joy of simply being with my friends and laughing together.

You are already familiar with some of the extreme things I did as I searched for my big life purpose. What you don't know is how much my impatience for a vision dominated my everyday life—even down to the music I played. During one period of time I listened to "Dream the Impossible Dream," "Climb Every Mountain," "When You Wish Upon a Star," and "Somewhere Over the Rainbow" nearly every day! Still, no vision.

Eventually I learned, much to my dismay, that there is no point in begging for a vision. God is the one who unveils it, and he has the option of doing so whenever he chooses. When we're in a big rush to receive our vision, we're simply trying to get ahead of God. We're arrogantly pushing through our agenda instead of prayerfully waiting for his clear direction. Our impatience never accelerates the revelation of his plan. We simply cannot demand vision.

WORTH THE WAIT

When Cathy, an elderly friend, was younger, she believed it was a waste of her time to wait for God to get around to initiating a dream in her life. Now, eight years into God's slow revelation of his plan for her, she has come to an amazing conclusion. She recognizes that the long period of waiting for God to reveal his vision and mobilize her was a much-needed step of preparation. The delay magnified the personal character issues she needed to address. It allowed her time to get to know all types of people and learn a variety of skills. Most important, it showed her the value of trusting God for his wisdom and timing.

If you are feeling impatient, as Cathy and I did, because of a long silence from God regarding his vision for your life, I have several suggestions. First, confess and repent of your impatience. Second, try thanking God for his wisdom in teaching you to wait for his good timing. And third, pay attention to what God is doing in your life *today*.

Let's explore this third suggestion a bit more. Do you recall the stepping-stone from chapter three of doing today what God sent you into the world to do? There we explored just how much our daily roles matter to God. He doesn't waste any part of a life dedicated to his ongoing purposes. While he does not always insist that a vision be preceded by faithfulness to our day-in, day-out purposes, those purposes can prepare us well to receive vision. What God is doing in your life today may directly support and prepare you for the vision he will reveal to you tomorrow.

> *For when your patience is finally in full bloom, then you will be ready for anything, strong in character, full and complete.*
> (JAMES 1:4, TLB)

Consider, for a moment, some of your routine, daily purposes, some of which are listed on the "Daily Purposes" side of the chart on the next page. You may have specific examples you would add to this list.

If you compare the level of godly service between the "Daily Purposes" and "God's Ultimate Vision," you can see a natural progression toward expanding effectiveness for God. Notice that while your daily purposes demand a high level of personal commitment to obeying God, vision escorts you to an interpersonal commitment of leading others to obey God. Vision moves you toward a singular life purpose of greater magnitude.

Daily Purposes	God's Ultimate Vision
Ministering to one or some	Ministering to some or multitudes
Working alone or alongside	Inviting others to participate
Expecting a tough assignment	Expecting God's intervention to complete an impossible assignment
Staying committed	Becoming sold out; no turning back
Saying, "Use me, God"	Praying boldly, "Use me up, God!"
Playing it safe and sure	Risking all; no holds barred
Making sense to you and others	Looking foolish in the eyes of the world
Handling daily tasks-at-hand in a Christlike manner	Carrying out your unique purpose in life filled with the fruit of the Spirit—love, joy, peace, patience, and so on

I have to admit it is pure genius on God's part to prepare us to hear his thoughts through years of daily roles, rather than to scare us half to death by announcing a full-fledged vision unexpectantly. More important, did you notice how a God-size vision could not possibly give us bragging rights? God's vision, given his way in his timing, accomplishes just the opposite: it causes us to drop to our knees in humility.

VISION REQUIRES ACTION

No matter how or when God's vision comes to you, your ideal response to the concept would be complete surrender followed by action. Many Christian women have surrendered their lives and received their vision, but they remain frozen in a state of inaction when it is time to actually accept God's call on their lives. Somewhat like being in the Indiana Jones movie, *The Last Crusade*, they stand immobile over the "Faith Gap," desperately wanting proof of safe passage, while God waits on the other side wanting them to trust him.

When I think of inaction, I think of Donna, a devout Christian, who first became aware of God's vision for her life during a spiritual retreat. She panicked at the enormity of it and pleaded, "Here I am, Lord, but send Alicia, not me!" (Her version of Isaiah 6:8!) Later, Donna tried a different tactic: "Lord, don't send me *there*. I'll go anywhere but *there*."

Have you ever blurted out similar appeals even though you knew the response God was hoping to hear? I have! Whenever we do that, we need to remember Jesus' words: "Why do you call me, 'Lord, Lord,' and do not do what I say?"[8]

Remember that God plays a powerful part in the unfolding of his plan. Of course our vision will be scary; a vision is supposed to be bigger than life, more complex, more far-reaching, more demanding than we know how to handle. When God gave Moses his vision, Moses wasn't sure he was the leader God seemed to think he was. But God assured Moses he was the man for the job. Then, God comforted Moses by saying, "I will certainly be with you."[9] Please realize that God gives *you* the same assurance of his presence during the completion of your life's work.

God is not looking for "superstars" to whom he can reveal a vision. He is looking for women in whom he can inspire a loving method of living and sharing the gospel. He is looking for dedicated, ordinary women who hold such a firm conviction about their unique purpose that they will doggedly persevere under trial.

> *Suddenly, the Spirit will emerge through the lives of ordinary people who hear a call and answer in extraordinary ways.*[10]
> ANN PETRIE,
> FILM PRODUCER
> AND DIRECTOR

Average Bible Folks Who Had Extraordinary Visions from God

The Bible is packed with examples of average folks to whom God gave extraordinary visions. Here's my paraphrase of the vision each received from God:

Noah, build an ark.[11]

Abram, go to the land I will show you.[12]

Sarah, you will be the mother of nations; kings of peoples will come from you.[13]

Joseph, you will reign over others.[14]

Moses, go to Pharaoh to demand that he let you lead my people out of Egypt.[15]

Joshua, get ready to cross the Jordan River.[16]

Deborah, go into battle; you will be victorious.[17]

Gideon, go in the strength you have, and save Israel.[18]

Esther, save your people.[19]

Jeremiah, go to everyone I send you to and say whatever I command you.[20]

Jonah, go to the great city of Nineveh and preach against it.[21]

Simon and Andrew, follow me.[22]

John the Baptist, prepare the way for me.[23]

Mary, you will be with child and give birth to a son, and you are to give him the name Jesus.[24]

Peter, feed my lambs.[25]

When God Is Ready, He Will Reveal His Vision!

Allow me to share how gently, persistently, and certainly God revealed his vision for my life. In 1988, I began to wonder if the vision God might have for me had something to do with nurturing seedlings. For years I didn't know what to make of that vague, incomplete idea that kept coming to mind. Then, in an instant one sunny day in 1991, I felt an overwhelming desire to help *something* grow so that it someday could be beautiful or useful. I had no clue whether God was asking me to care for orchids, soy beans, cactus plants, or oak trees! I simply knew that I wanted what I was feeling—the sense of having been handed a faint, yet splendid, idea—to come true. Strangely enough, I wanted it more than anything in the whole world (other than the continued spiritual growth, safety, and health of my two children).

I felt that being part of a planting process would make me burst with joy, but that was the extent of my ability to comprehend the details at the time. I knew for sure that something was brewing in my heart, but I could see it only as if through a fog. I could never quite get a handle on it. I definitely couldn't verbalize it because I was afraid people might think I was daft.

I had no idea how to process the thoughts of seeds, flowers, fruits, and planting that were running through my mind. I knew nothing back then of the hundreds of Bible verses God would later have me study that have to do with gardens, grain, vineyards, fields, harvest, plowing, pruning, seasons, sprouting, budding, and blossoming. I began to wonder if the images of seeds, planting, and growth had a literal meaning such as "Go purchase a flower shop" or "Go into the career of horticulture" or "Find a farmer to marry!" That's how bewildered I felt.

It was not until 1994, six years after the ideas first began to form, that God made the vision clear. All along, he slowly had been depositing in my soul distinct sensory images and impressions of his future plans for me. At last it was time for him to reveal the purpose that would hold my heart gratefully captive forever. Finally I could identify the passionate ache in my heart. It was my life's purpose, the search for which had driven me crazy for years. The now-obvious work God had assigned to me was this: to help women grow into all God intended them to be, and to help them come into full bloom for him in order to glorify him with their lives!

But how was I supposed to do that? Well, answers unfolded as I needed them. I now know that I am to help women understand the stepping-stones such as peace, love, and surrender that will lead them down the pathway to purpose. It is almost as if God had been laying out stepping-stones one at a time for me to field test. I now fulfill God's vision for my life by pointing women down the pathway toward Jesus— to his magnificence and his purposes.

Don't ask me why God gave me this particular vision. For me it is a fascinating purpose that I love beyond all measure. It makes my heart sing. Receiving God's vision feels like Christmas morning when you get the perfect gift for you—perhaps, a miniature poodle—and I get the perfect gift for me—a multicolored, thousand-piece puzzle. (If you don't ask me to kiss your poodle, I won't ask you to work on my puzzle!) God gives each of us something that makes us smile in ministry, and he will surround us as needed with like-minded people to help us complete the unique purpose he has reserved for us on earth.

I had lived through a torturous, tedious, and tearful process of self-doubt, endless prayer, relentless perseverance, testing the waters of service in many areas, jaunts around the world to talk to famous people, and the pouring out of my heart to strangers and friends. I had searched for a long time before God more fully revealed to me my individual, long-term purpose. His clarity was not available to me one nanosecond earlier or later. I'm convinced the reason he did not make it easy on me was so that I would be passionately motivated to encourage other women who are selected for the long, long, long process.

EPIPHANY

The magi, the wise men of the East, recognized the manifestation of Christ's divine nature when they brought him presents suitable for a king. It is one of the times in the Bible that is referred to as an *epiphany*, a moment when God clearly revealed himself. You recall that familiar Christmas story:

> And look! The star appeared to them [the kings] again, standing over Bethlehem. Their joy knew no bounds! Entering the house where the baby and Mary his mother were, they threw themselves down before him, worshiping. Then they opened their presents and gave him gold, frankincense and myrrh.[26]

What if God caused an epiphany in your life today? What if he boldly disclosed to you more about his character and his ways? What if he demonstrated clearly who he is and how you can worship him with your life? What if he explained to you why he made you and what far-reaching purpose he has always had in mind specifically for you? What if he unveiled to you what gift you will give to Jesus and, in return, what gifts he will give to you and to his people through you? I am sure you would bow before the King and magnify him even more than you do now. Your joy would know no bounds. It would be a moment of extreme celebration.

If you have not already received God's vision for your life, it is important that you prepare for and expect an epiphany. Perhaps you will have a sneak preview, a series of impressions, as I experienced for six years about growing something. Perhaps vision will come with little warning. In any case, Jesus Christ wants to be made manifest in your life. He wants to make it obvious who he is and what he would like to see happen in your life. At the best time for you, and for the people he will send you to serve, he will invite you to an epiphany. In the meantime, just keep putting one foot in front of the other on the pathway to purpose.

Although God wants us to prepare ourselves to receive his vision, he can send a vision at any time—even if we haven't asked for it and others don't think we are ready for it. He sometimes interrupts our lives and works in unexpected ways as he did in the life of Saul, who later became the missionary Paul. Consider Saul's blinding-light conversion and epiphany described in Acts:

> We all fell to the ground, and I heard a voice saying to me in Aramaic, "Saul, Saul, why do you persecute me? . . ."
>
> Then I asked, "Who are you, Lord?"
>
> "I am Jesus, whom you are persecuting," the Lord replied. "Now get up and stand on your feet. I have appeared to you to appoint you as a servant and as a witness of what you have seen of me and what I will show you. . . . I am sending you to them to open their eyes . . . so that they may receive forgiveness of sins. . . ."
>
> So then . . . I was not disobedient to the vision from heaven.[27]

Most of us don't receive a dramatic, blinding vision like Saul did. Instead, we are given a sneak preview of God's direction for our lives as a childhood fantasy, a youthful wish, or a passionate longing. So pay attention to any "seedling" ideas you might be sensing or to an emboldened version of a career or ministry you currently love. Be particularly aware and receptive to impressions you get through prayer, reading your Bible, journaling, Christian teachers, mentors, and role models. These may be God's way of revealing his thoughts to you.

THE SOJOURNER'S GUIDE TO RECEIVING GOD'S VISION

The following suggestions are intended to help you prepare yourself to listen for God's thoughts and receive his vision for your life. Patiently continue these practices for as long as necessary.

Pray

The best thing to do while you anticipate God's revelation of a vision for your life is to pray. Pray that you will hear God and be made pliable in his hands. While you are waiting, ask him which of the stepping-stones you may need to revisit so that you are better prepared to receive his vision. Pray too for God's perfect timing, that he will ready the hearts of the people he is sending you to serve. You may also benefit from another book in this series, *Praying for Purpose for Women.*

Ask Others to Pray

Surround yourself with loving, supportive people who will pray with you regarding God's vision for your life. Ask them to pray specifically that you will be receptive to God's best for you. Another book in this series, *Conversations on Purpose for Women,* is designed to help you talk openly and pray about your unique life purpose with a "Purpose Partner," a woman to whom you can entrust your impressions of God's plans for your life.

Be Confident

Confidence means "with faith." For this step, you need faith that will move mountains, faith that will unleash the power of God. You must believe that God will cast the vision he has always had for you! Talk to him about nurturing your faith so his vision for your life will become apparent to you.

Practice Patience

Practice waiting graciously in all of your daily activities, including standing in line at the bank or grocery store. Practice patience by engaging in activities that require it, perhaps flying a kite or planting a garden. In addition, take time to sing, play, and relax so you can learn to slow down and enjoy the journey.

Ask God Specifically to Speak to You

If you think you want God to speak to you, you may want to ask yourself two very important questions: *Do I really want and expect God to speak to me?* and *Am I really listening?* If your answer is yes to both questions, you are ready to echo the prayer of Samuel: "Speak, for your servant is listening."[28]

> ### Recommended Books on God's Vision
>
> *Experiencing God: Knowing and Doing the Will of God,*
> by Henry T. Blackaby and Claude V. King[29]
> *Living the Life You Were Meant to Live,* by Tom Paterson[30]

Now Is the Time to See God's Boldest Vision for Your Life

Proverbs is clear that "where there is no vision, the people perish."[31] In recognition of this basic fact of human behavior, some corporations have created the job of Vice President of Vision Access. The funny thing is, in God's eyes all of us are VPs of Vision Access because he intends each us to have access to his vision for our lives!

So will you take this next step toward God and his purpose for your life? Will you *eagerly anticipate that the Lord God Almighty will reveal his vision to you*? Our sweet Savior is waiting for each Christian woman, not just a select few, to accept the vision he has endearingly crafted for her. Are you willing to accept whatever vision God has prepared and will reveal to you? Will you thank him before, during, and after the revelation of his vision?

If you haven't yet received God's vision, if you haven't yet heard his exact instructions, don't you dare give up! God has been in the vision business from the very beginning of time and he is not going to quit now. Don't be shy about requesting access to his vision. When the timing is right, he will reveal more about who he is and what he has reserved for you to do.

When your long-awaited day of epiphany comes, when God presents you with his vision, rejoice! You may want to fall on your knees in worship and pray:

Dear Lord, keep me close to you. I love you and cannot begin to fulfill this vision apart from you. I need your inspiration, insight, humility, wisdom, truth, knowledge, understanding, patience, stamina, humor, direction, answers, style, skill, sensitivity, clarification, holiness, and love. Don't leave me, not even for a second. Thank you for sharing your thoughts with me. Thank you for revealing your purpose-filled vision for my life. Amen.

GOD'S WISDOM FOR THE PATHWAY

THE "DEBORAH" STEP OF LIFE: EAGERLY ANTICIPATE THAT THE LORD GOD ALMIGHTY WILL REVEAL HIS VISION TO YOU

For a lesson from Deborah, prophetess and judge, during this step of your life, read her story in Judges 4 and the celebratory *Song of Deborah* in Judges 5. Deborah was the only known female judge of Israel, and she was characterized by her wisdom.

Jabin, the king of Canaan, and Sisera, the commander of the king's army, had terrorized Israel for twenty years. Deborah summoned Barak, her countryman, in the name of Yahweh, and informed him that God would deliver the enemy into his hands. Barak refused to go unless Deborah went with him. She did go, and the enemy was soundly defeated. Expect God to give you a clear vision, like he gave Deborah.

Personal Pathway Question

Without analyzing your answer, quickly jot down in your spiritual journal *what you'd like to think* God's vision for you is.

If you are not able to answer this question right now, please don't worry about it. As you know from reading this book, a wide variety of clarifying work is involved. Look back over your responses to the questions at the end of each chapter to help you determine your next action step. Trust me that the intentional work you do now will invite an answer. Also, don't forget to rest in the Lord, pray, and believe that God will reveal his plan for you.

NOTES

1. (p. 185) See Daniel 2:28, NLT.
2. (p. 185) See 1 Samuel 3:1–18; Isaiah 6:1–13.
3. (p. 185) See Mark 12:30–31.
4. (p. 185) See Matthew 28:18–20.
5. (p. 187) Isaiah 55:2, NKJV.
6. (p. 187) Isaiah 55:3, NKJV.
7. (p. 188) Patrick M. Morley, *Seven Seasons of a Man's Life* (Nashville: Thomas Nelson, 1995), 229.
8. (p. 191) Luke 6:46.
9. (p. 191) Exodus 3:12, TLB.
10. (p. 191) Ann Petrie's words used in the film, *Mother Teresa*, by Petrie Productions, Inc. Narration by Richard Attenborough. Produced and directed by Jeanette and Ann Petrie, 1986.
11. (p. 192) See Genesis 6:12–14.
12. (p. 192) See Genesis 12:1–3.
13. (p. 192) See Genesis 17:15–16.
14. (p. 192) See Genesis 37:1–11.
15. (p. 192) See Exodus 3:10.
16. (p. 192) See Joshua 1:1–2.
17. (p. 192) See Judges 4:1–14.
18. (p. 192) See Judges 6:12–16.
19. (p. 192) See Esther 4:14.
20. (p. 192) See Jeremiah 1:4–8.
21. (p. 192) See Jonah 1:1–2.
22. (p. 192) See Mark 1:16–17.
23. (p. 192) See Luke 1:13–17.
24. (p. 192) See Luke 1:26–33.
25. (p. 192) See John 21:15.
26. (p. 195) Matthew 2:9–11, TLB.
27. (p. 196) Acts 26:14–19.
28. (p. 197) 1 Samuel 3:10.
29. (p. 198) Henry T. Blackaby and Claude V. King, *Experiencing God: Knowing and Doing the Will of God (The Workbook)* (Nashville: Lifeway, 1990).
30. (p. 198) Tom Paterson, *Living the Life You Were Meant to Live* (Nashville: Thomas Nelson, 1998).
31. (p. 198) Proverbs 29:18, KJV.

Chapter 12

TAKE COURAGE

But Jesus immediately said to them [his disciples]:
"Take courage! It is I. Don't be afraid."
(MATTHEW 14:27)

As we continue on the pathway to purpose, some women will laugh out loud at the sight of our next stepping-stone, *take courage*. We can't begin to imagine how we can muster the courage to tackle a God-sized life purpose. But the good news is that we don't have to muster anything. Courage is a gift from God. To receive it, we need only show up and rely upon God's complete faithfulness.

The stepping-stone of courage is not a mere pebble in the stream that we hope will keep us from falling in and getting wet. It is much more like the Rock of Gibraltar, a spectacular, towering limestone promontory. We can think of it as God's secure, safe haven for us. It is his message, "Trust me," that beckons us to step forward with courage.

GOD'S GIFT OF COURAGE

Can you imagine trying to handle the fears that can accompany a bigger-than-life purpose without access to God's place of safety? I can't! Not for a minute. I need plenty of courage to fulfill God's purpose for my life, and my guess is that you do too. So let's explore the kind of courage God offers us.

The gospel writer Matthew describes the step of taking courage as a *directive* from Jesus. That means that Jesus *commands* that we be fearless. This is not to say that God can never use us to accomplish his purposes if we are afraid. He can and he does. And it doesn't mean that if we take this step of courage all of our fears will magically vanish. What it does mean is that taking courage is a determined act of our will that helps us release our fears and enables us to move forward. Taking courage is an act we initiate that is based on something real and reliable—God's steadfastness.

Taking courage begins with our understanding that the Lord God has called each of us by name and promises to be with us. The prophet Isaiah explains this concept best when he reminds us that we are precious and honored in God's sight, that we are loved, and that our heavenly Father will never leave us nor forsake us:

> Fear not, for I have redeemed you;
> I have summoned you by name;
> you are mine.
> When you pass through the waters,
> I will be with you;
> and when you pass through the rivers,
> they will not sweep over you.
> When you walk through the fire,
> you will not be burned;
> the flames will not set you ablaze.
> For I am the LORD, your God . . .
> You are precious and honored in my sight . . .
> Do not be afraid, for I am with you.[1]

This description of God's love for us and his promise to be with us gives me great comfort and peace of mind. It explains why I have no reason to fear—God is with me! So even when I *feel* afraid, I can persevere because God has promised to be with me. As I begin to grasp the truth of his presence with me, I can exhale with relief and move forward with courage.

Jesus vividly illustrated the same message to his disciples while he was with them on earth. In the darkness of a stormy night, the disciples were in a boat that was being tossed about by violent waves. Jesus appeared to them on the water, and the already frightened disciples became terrified that he was a ghost. How did Jesus respond? He said, "Take courage! It is I. Don't be afraid."[2]

There is no reason to be afraid when Jesus is with us! How comforting it is to know that Jesus is the one who encourages us like he did Peter that night. He calls us to step out of the boat and walk on the water toward him, as he reaches out his hand to catch us when we start to sink under the fearful pressures of life. He is the reason we can be fearless. Whether our fears vanish or whether we press on toward our goal even though we are afraid, we will receive courage as we obey God and experience his faithfulness.

WHY IS COURAGE SO IMPORTANT?

All of us are vulnerable to being sidetracked by fear. One of the unexpected findings in my interviews with the macho young men I visited in prison (see chapter six) was that they all lived in fear of something. And, I know from personal experience long ago how immobilizing it is to be wrapped in layers of fear that cause worry. Now, as I coach women toward their life purposes, I sometimes see women whose secret fears of flying, abandonment, public speaking, heights, rejection, being attacked, and so on have prevented them from being all God designed them to be.

There is no doubt in my mind that fear impacts life purpose. I know how detrimental it can be in the lives of Christians who are attempting to live out God's purpose for their lives. Once fear has you in its wicked grasp, it blocks creativity, productivity, and relationships. So when you face your fears by grasping onto God's courage, you regain your capacity for experiencing these things as you live out your life purpose.

More important, as you obediently take courage, your view of God's faithfulness and power will increase. You see, God wants to calm your fears so that your relationship with him will be more trusting and intimate. The more you trust him, the more you live with the assurance that he is in control. As your relationship with him deepens, you become more and more willing to be entrusted with bold and difficult opportunities to serve him.

I know that taking courage when we face fear is not easy, but the effort is always worth the freedom that results. God will honor your courage and dedication. His gift of courage is like getting out of jail free. So let's consider some of the more common fears that can sidetrack us from pursuing God's purposes, and let's explore how we might take courage when we encounter those fears.

Fear of Ridicule and Criticism

Do you have a fear of ridicule or criticism that keeps you from pursuing your purpose? Do you say, "Others will laugh at me. They'll make cruel jokes about my values, beliefs, ethics, and morals. What if they confront me, and I don't know how to defend myself?"

I know this fear well. For years it kept me from evangelism. I was terrified that someone would criticize the core beliefs I hold so dear or would embarrass me about my poor recall of Scripture. But one day I asked myself a crucial question: *Do I really intend to let somebody's comments or criticism keep me from stepping out in faith to do the work God gave me to do?* When I thought about it that way, the answer was "Of course not!" I wanted to fulfill God's purpose for my life, so I had to choose to take courage and do the work he had given me even though I was afraid.

Fear of Success

You may not recognize it immediately, but fear of success can also paralyze you and prevent you from fulfilling your life purpose. It may cause you to torture yourself with thoughts such as: *If I succeed, people will be jealous and won't include me anymore. Success will make me stand out in the crowd, and that's the last thing I want. I'll have to live up to other people's expectations of me, and I won't be able to coast anymore. Besides, I really don't deserve to succeed. And, success might make me swell up with pride.*

Fear of success not only makes you easy prey for those who are not on fire with God's vision and think unaffirming thoughts about you, but it also makes you easy prey for your own imagination about what they might think. The best thing you can do to counteract this fear is to recognize that true success is only what God views as success, not what others think or say.

Fear of Being Found Out

Being *found out* is a common fear that I refer to as the "impostor syndrome." It is an excessive concern that people will figure out that you're not really smart enough, good enough, funny enough, articulate enough, organized enough, or loving enough to really fulfill God's purpose for your life. I have seen this fear grow to epidemic proportions among women.

What do impostors do? Many of them work as hard as they can for as long as they can until they give up trying to hide their darkest secret or trying to prove themselves capable to the rest of the world. It is utterly exhausting to worry that the *real you* will be exposed, thus confirming that God chose the wrong gal to tackle the life purpose he intended for you. I know from personal and professional experience that the day a woman decides to quit being an impostor is the happiest day of her life.

You can stumble only if you're moving.
ANONYMOUS

I remember well my fear of being found out after I was laid off and spent fourteen months securing a new job. Although I was doing excellent work for my new employer, I dreaded the day when someone would find out I wasn't competent enough or productive enough. Instead of seeking to fulfill my daily purposes in a way that pleased God, I directed my energy into being a boss-pleasing impostor.

I will be forever grateful to a good friend who showed me a practical way to take courage in that situation. He insisted that I write down examples of how well God had provided for my kids and me while I was jobless. As I began to remember and record God's miracles in my life, I saw how God had been with me all along—just as he promised he would be. That evidence of God's faithfulness in my life infused me with courage and allowed me to enjoy my new job.

Fear of Failure

One of the most all-consuming fears is the fear of failure. Have you ever said, "If I fail, nobody will ever believe in me again. I'll look like a fool. People will think I'm stupid because I can't get it right. People will whisper, 'She fell flat on her face. I guess that will teach her to get so far out there'"? If so, you have plenty of company.

Many people view personal failure as if it were the AIDS virus—life-threatening, devastating, and too sad to discuss. But the fact is, we *will* fail, and God graciously will offer to forgive us for our shortcomings. So I hope by this point on the pathway that you have learned to put your failures in perspective and to keep walking forward in spite of them. If God can forgive us, why not take courage and forgive yourself for your mistakes—past, present, and future?

> *Failure foreshadows success.*
> ANONYMOUS

No matter what our fears, the only way we can create a place secure from fear is to do nothing and go nowhere. What a narrow margin of living space that leaves us! We will perish either from lethargy or claustrophobia. So if you find yourself living in a tiny, fear-enclosed box about what God is asking you to do with your life today, here's an idea—pray for claustrophobia! At least that way your instinct will be to break out! Seriously, accept God's forgiveness and ask him to help you step out of the box.

COURAGEOUS WOMEN GIVE ME HOPE!

I am grateful to the many courageous women I know of who did not let fear of rejection or failure stop them. I'd like to share with you the stories of three remarkable women who conquered fear.

Queen Elizabeth I: Her father cursed her at birth because she was a girl. The Pope declared her illegitimate, and her half-sister imprisoned her in the Tower of London. Later in life, Elizabeth reigned as queen for forty-five years, during which time England grew in prosperity, peace, and power. She instituted the right to a fair trial and pioneered social welfare programs for the elderly, infirm, and poor.

Elizabeth Blackwell: Twenty-nine medical colleges rejected her before she became America's first woman doctor. After several hospitals refused to hire her, she opened the New York Infirmary for Indigent Women and Children. Later, she founded a women's medical college.

Mary McLeod Bethune: She was the youngest of seventeen children. When she was turned down for missionary service, she started a school instead. Her students used boxes for desks and elderberries for ink. To raise money she and her students hauled thousands of pounds of garbage for a local dump owner. President Franklin Roosevelt distinguished Mary as the first African-American woman to be a presidential adviser.

> *Always too soon to quit. Never too late to start.*
> ANONYMOUS

These women of courage help give me hope to tackle the difficult ministry and mission tasks God assigns to me. I don't know how they conquered the fears they faced, but I do know that I would love to impact the world, as they did, in spite of my fears!

COURAGE DEFICIT

One day in Calcutta, my mom and I mustered enough courage to volunteer at the Home for Dying Destitutes. We traveled there via a wild rickshaw ride, weaving precariously through the free-for-all streets, and a dangerous subway ride where pickpockets prey upon tourists in the crowds. Our fellow volunteers made sure we stayed alert during every minute of the commute.

India's public transportation did not turn out to be as threatening as we had feared. The Home for the Dying, however, turned out to be far more frightening than we had anticipated. After reporting to the volunteer desk, my mom and I washed our hands and put on our already soiled aprons. We were invited to take a few minutes to acclimate to our new surroundings and then to report for afternoon chores. A Sister of Charity informed us that we would be bathing and feeding several of the women, and asked us to choose our first patient. My mom and I pasted quivering smiles on our faces, locked arms, and stoically strolled down the entire length of the women's ward. We were trying to get oriented, trying to connect with the dying strangers, trying to find some semblance of hope—and, frankly, trying to stall.

Nothing in my life had come close to preparing me to minister to the dying. The smell of death was in the air. Tears of panic stung my eyes. Even my mom, who had been an army nurse under General Patton, looked terrified. I couldn't believe my inability to cope with the situation. As I prayed that God would calm my trembling and anxious heart, I began to question my sanity for ever thinking that I would make a good, short-term, lay missionary. How had I made the mistake of agreeing to this horrifying volunteer work?

Finally I was relieved to see an attractive, smiling woman lying on the last cot. Her eyes met mine. I eagerly announced to the supervising Sister that we would like to spend some time talking with and perhaps feeding this patient—but heavens no, not bathing her. And, just to make sure the ground rules were clear, I added that we would not be clipping her toenails!

The wise Sister whispered, "Not a good choice. Pick someone else. This patient has advanced consumption . . . you know, tuberculosis."

That was all I needed to hear. Even though I had had all the shots required for international travel, the reality of the clear and present danger—that I might catch a life-threatening disease—came thundering down on me and disabled me. My mom and I, communicating in our unspoken mother-daughter language, made an executive decision: it was time to sneak away. Filled with fear, we escaped up the back stairs to the rooftop. Once outside, we gulped in the fresh air and decided to remain there for the rest of our shift.

I was in shock. Guilt attacked me. Why couldn't I do this special assignment of ministering to several dying women for a few hours? Why was I such a huge Christian failure all the time? Couldn't I get any ministry right? How could God ever trust me with a broader life purpose if I couldn't even give a stranger a cup of cold water in his name? I burst into tears and blamed myself with the condemning words, "What's wrong with me?"

Within minutes an angel, in the human form of a long-term volunteer who was on her rosary break, approached us. When I saw her, I thought she would reprimand us for deserting our post. I began searching for a defense, struggling to recall whether there was a commandment, "Thou shalt feed and bathe the dying." My mom and I were so upset by what we had seen downstairs that we simultaneously began rambling off excuses for our behavior with sentence fragments like: "Uh . . . don't feel well . . . pager went off . . . scenic view of the city on the rooftop."

The dear woman smiled and asked us to tell her what was on our minds. My mom nodded for me to take the lead and tell our visitor why I had come to Calcutta. The volunteer patiently answered my questions about life, inner peace, spiritual readiness, godly goals, and finding my purpose in life. She listened and told us that Jesus understood our fear. She did not condemn us for sitting out the rest of our shift. Her timeless words of advice still echo in my ears: "Take what you have seen and put it to good use back in the States and in your own home. Think with your heart, not with your head so much. Walk in other people's shoes, and see life from their perspective. It is only in loving them that you can serve them."[3]

Although she was a stranger to me, that woman's warmth and generosity had spiritually bathed and fed me when I lacked the courage to physically bathe or feed others. She told me that I could search out simple service opportunities to do for and with my family and in my own community. Furthermore, she assured me that God would make my calling clear, so I was no longer to be concerned about the details of where, how, when, or even if he would ask me to serve him in a grand and dramatic fashion. And most emphatically, she said that I was to cherish my current roles in life.

When I got back to the United States, I began to do the homework she recommended, and I learned about thinking with my heart instead of my head. As I did that deliberate work, God grew my faith and gave me newfound courage. It's as if God were a banker who entered my fear on his ledger as a debit, then *wiped my debt clean*, added some extra funds, and cashed me out with a credit of courage! It is not logical, but who am I to question God?

I don't know what fears stop you cold in your tracks. Whatever they may be, I urge you to take a step of courage each time. The Lord said, "Have I not commanded you? Be strong and courageous. Do not be terrified; do not be discouraged, for the LORD your God will be with you wherever you go."[4] God has promised to be with you. Nothing beats taking hold of his hand as you walk through fear, shouting, "God struck down Goliath for me today, and all is well."

Did you know that God does not need our courage to proceed with his plans? We can pick any one of a number of Bible stories—Jonah, Moses, Esther, or Peter, for example—and see that God accomplished his work in the midst of someone's fear. So, we really have only two choices when it comes to fears related to fulfilling our life purpose. The first is to complete God's assignments while kicking and screaming in fear. And our second choice is to make the entire journey easier by beginning today to give our fears to God, or at least to trust that he is with us as we do his work.

THE SOJOURNER'S GUIDE TO TAKING COURAGE

The following suggestions will help you step securely on the rock of courage. Take as much time as you need to complete the steps that are most helpful to you, and repeat them as often as necessary to continue stepping forward with courage.

Use the Fear Hierarchy Approach

Make a list of all the things you fear about living out God's purposes for your life. Are you afraid he will send you to Africa as a missionary? Are you afraid you will somehow fall short of God's intentions? Are you afraid you will anger someone who liked your previous status quo or that you will be called a Jesus Freak? Are you afraid that you will need to repent of a pet sin in your life or work on your character? Are you afraid you will not have enough money for the task or that you will have to quit your job? Are you afraid you will have to give up your current ministry, join a Bible study, meet a stranger, or invite a neighbor to church? Or, are you afraid you will have to encounter and wrestle with the existential fear that life has no ultimate meaning? No matter what your fears are, rank them in order from least to worst.

Pray over your list, and ask others to pray on your behalf that God will reveal the truth about your fears as they relate to his purpose for you. Then, take a stand and boldly claim God's promise that he will be with you. Next, take a baby step and offer one of your lesser fears to God. Keep working the list, fear by fear, for as long as it takes. Reward yourself each time you overcome a fear. (No, not a shopping or food reward!)

Ask Yourself Two Questions

First, ask yourself, "How does fear keep me focused on myself?" Write down your answer and review it in a week. If it fills you with a godly sorrow, repent of your self-focus.

Second, ask yourself, "What has fear stolen from me?" (for example, an opportunity for God to bless me or for me to bless God or others).

Discuss your answer with a friend and ask for advice on how to take courage against your fears.

Apply the "Just Eat Your Spinach" Approach

My sister, my son, and I use the "just eat your spinach" approach to coax each other through frightening assignments, and it really works for us. You might want to try it—if you hate spinach as much as we do! Here's the gist of it: Sometimes you just have to go ahead and eat your dreaded *spinach*—by giving your first speech, by presenting your idea for a novel, or by making your difficult request—before you have time to smell and taste the awful stuff called fear. Sometimes the best course of action is to just "go for it," even when you're afraid of what is ahead. Trust God to see you through.

Feed Your Courage with the Word of God

There are plenty of courage-building passages in Scripture. Here are just a few from the Psalms that you won't want to miss. Read them, meditate on them, and journal about them.

> I will not fear the tens of thousands drawn up against me on every side (Psalm 3:6, context verses 5–7).

> Even though I walk through the valley of the shadow of death, I will fear no evil, for you are with me; your rod and your staff, they comfort me (Psalm 23:4, context verses 3–5).

> Though an army besiege me, my heart will not fear; though war break out against me, even then will I be confident (Psalm 27:3, context verses 2–4).

> I sought the LORD, and he answered me; he delivered me from all my fears (Psalm 34:4, context verses 3–5).

> Therefore we will not fear, though the earth give way and the mountains fall into the heart of the sea (Psalm 46:2, context verses 1–3).

You will not fear the terror of night, nor the arrow that flies by
day (Psalm 91:5, context verses 4–6).

He will have no fear of bad news; his heart is steadfast, trusting in
the LORD (Psalm 112:7, context verses 6–8).

RECOMMENDED BOOKS ON COURAGE

Feeling Secure in a Troubled World, by Charles Stanley[5]
Women of Courage, by Debra Evans[6]

NOW IS THE TIME TO ASK FOR COURAGE

We had a family cat that we called Fraidy Cat because she was
spooked by everything. She hid like a fugitive on the run, disappearing
for days without a trace, except for the cat food missing from her bowl.
In rare moments, she graced us with her presence—only to go screech-
ing back into hiding when the doorbell chimed, the phone rang, a lawn
mower started up outside, or an unfamiliar voice spoke.

That phantom pet is a perfect picture of how fear-prone people
sometimes act. Like our cat, they follow a run-and-hide pattern. Would
you like to quit running and hiding from your deepest fears? Are you
willing to give God the fears you have about living out his purposes? Are
you ready to take this next step toward God and his purpose for your
life? Are you ready to *take courage*?

Janet Congo, a dear friend of mine, has this to say about fear in *Free
to Be God's Woman*:

Positive Christian women move out even when their knees are shaking.
Why? Because they have been kneeling on those knees that are shaking. Not only do they know *who* they are, they know *whose* they are.[7]

Although your knees may be shaking, will you trust your kind God
to reveal more about himself to you and to accomplish his purposes

through you today and tomorrow? Is now the time to get rid of your fear of ridicule, your fear of success or failure, your fear of not being good enough, or whatever your pet fear is? To walk through fear, you have to choose to break out of the self-defeating box that limits you and your perception of God. Are you ready to be God's courageous woman? He is beckoning you to trust him and take courage. There is no better time than now to begin.

GOD'S WISDOM FOR THE PATHWAY

THE "ESTHER" STEP OF LIFE: TAKE COURAGE

For a lesson on courage from Queen Esther for this step of your life, read Esther 1–10. Esther was called upon to risk her life in order to save her Jewish people, and she responded that she would take the risk, saying, "If I perish, I perish." If God gave you a bold assignment today that caused you to be afraid, would you carry it to completion, no matter what? Would you, like Esther, pray and do a spiritual fast (and ask others to do the same) before you began? Ask God to give you his power to obey him, when you can't get over your fears, so that nothing interferes with what he has in mind for you both now and later.

Personal Pathway Questions

1. What are your greatest fears about your life purposes?

2. Which fears, if any, have you successfully released to the power of God?

3. What is God nudging you to do about one or more of your fears?

4. What is your response to this quote from pastor Adrian Rogers: "Don't be afraid of the will of God. The will of God will not take you where the power of God cannot keep you"?[8]

NOTES

1. (p. 204) Isaiah 43:1–5.
2. (p. 205) Matthew 14:27, see also verses 25–33.
3. (p. 211) Conversation with the author on the rooftop of Home for Dying Destitutes, Calcutta, India, 3 December 1987.
4. (p. 212) Joshua 1:9.
5. (p. 215) Charles Stanley, *Feeling Secure in a Troubled World* (Nashville: Thomas Nelson, 2000).
6. (p. 215) Debra Evans, *Women of Courage* (Grand Rapids: Zondervan, 2000).
7. (p. 215) Janet Congo, *Free to Be God's Woman* (Ventura, Calif.: Regal, 1985), 148.
8. (p. 217) Adrian Rogers, *Back to the Basics: Volume 2* audio series, "How to Know the Will of God" (Memphis: Love Worth Finding Ministries, 1994).

Chapter 13

BRING GLORY TO GOD

*[Jesus prayed,] "I have brought you glory on earth
by completing the work you gave me to do."*
(JOHN 17:1, 4)

Remember the faraway vistas you saw when you began your journey on the pathway to purpose? Now they are just a step away! One final leap, and your life becomes part of the inviting landscape you longed for from the other side of the stream. The step you are about to take is truly the most miraculous and joyous step of all: *bring glory to God by completing the work he gave you to do.*

You see, you are a *poiēma*, "God's workmanship."[1] You are his magnificent *magnum opus*, a precious masterpiece of enormous love. He ingeniously wove you together before you were born, perfectly fitting you for a broad-reach, soul-engaging purpose that would display his glory. And you can offer God no greater worship than to magnify him with your entire life.

But you must decide whether you will pursue God's vision for your life and glorify him through it. It is your choice. God will be glorified regardless of whether or not you choose to match step with him and fulfill your life purpose. His glory is never dependent on you or me, but what an incredible privilege we have to choose to participate in his work on earth. What an honor God gives us by allowing us to revere him with every step we take through life!

I think Bach, the composer, understood this concept as well as anyone. He is widely known for adding to his musical compositions the inscription *SDG*, the Latin initials for *soli deo gloria*, which in English means, "to God alone be the glory." How about you? Do you desire to exalt God with every action you take? Are you eager to add the inscription *SDG* to your life's symphony?

HOW CAN YOU POSSIBLY COMPLETE THE TASK?

Once you have caught sight of God's vision and accepted his big life purpose for you, it is perfectly normal to wonder how you are to accomplish the task God has assigned to you. You may question whether it is even possible. Despite the enormity of the job before you, let me assure you it *is* possible. Jesus even told us how to accomplish it in Matthew 11:29–30: "Walk with me and work with me—watch how I do it. Learn the unforced rhythms of grace. I won't lay anything heavy or ill-fitting on you. Keep company with me and you'll learn to live freely and lightly" (MSG).

> *"I knew you before you were formed within your mother's womb; before you were born I sanctified you and appointed you as my spokesman to the world."*
> (JEREMIAH 1:5, TLB)

Jesus is our example of how to do what God asks of us. While he was doing his Father's work on earth, Jesus continually prayed to him for guidance and strength so that he could complete the huge task before him. God's custom-made purpose for us also demands that we ask for his power and grace because of the difficult and varied aspects of the work he has entrusted to us. But the pressure to complete God's work isn't actually on us; it is on God! He is the one who knows what we are to do. He is the one who will provide the strength and resources.

Walking and working with God is like having a personal navigation system that keeps us going in the right direction. God knows where he wants us to go and how he wants us to get there. Our responsibility is simply to show up and say, "Hi, God, I've shown up for work today. How can I serve you? What would you like me to do next? What path have you laid out for me to follow? What resources, strength, and relationships have you prepared for me?"

God has always known the exact moment of your birth and death. He will not give you more than you can accomplish before he takes you home. If you focus on staying on track with your life purpose, God will enable you to carry out your portion of his work while you are on earth. This is true whether you are currently accomplishing your purpose on a dead run or taking your first steps to prepare yourself, your character, your finances, your network, or your skills for what lies ahead.

As you consider what needs to happen in your life for you to follow God's plan, guard against losing hope because of the many unknowns. Instead, focus on what you do know and trust him with the details. You can look forward to much less compartmentalization of your time, energy, resources, spiritual growth, talents, character, experiences, and roles as you practice a laserlike concentration

> *A focused person behaves far differently from a person without focus. Life has much more meaning, much more purpose, much more intensity. If we focus deeply enough, we bring the subject of our focus to a point of centeredness. This principle can be seen clearly in the way a lens can be used to concentrate and intensify the rays of the sun.*[2]
> TOM PATERSON

with your highly amplified life calling and focused destiny. What a party of purpose and joy God must have planned for those who are faithful to complete his work!

As is true on any job, some of us will get a late start, others will take long breaks at the water cooler, and some will squeeze in a game of golf in the afternoon. Despite our deliberate delays as well as life's unexpected setbacks, Jesus' model is for us to accomplish the task we have been given. No matter how impossible that task looks today, boldly take your next step forward for the glory of God. Look forward to the day when he congratulates you for doing what he gave you to do while you were on earth. Look forward to his words, "Well done, good and faithful servant!"[3]

DISCOVERING A JOY YOU HAVE NEVER KNOWN

What a joy it will be to hear those words of appreciation and approval from our Lord when our life on earth is done! But we don't have to wait until heaven to experience joy. God rewards us with joy as we fulfill his will. Let me share a bit about how we experience that joy.

The best way to faithfully accomplish the work of God is by committing heart and soul to Jesus. As we walk with him to fulfill our purpose and carry out his plans, we come to know Jesus like never before! The natural result of that intimate knowledge of Jesus is joy. As we get to know him, we understand more and more why the angels sang "joy to the world" when he was born!

Joy can be defined as colossal pleasure or intense satisfaction that fills us with gladness. True joy is not based on our circumstances. It is based on our acknowledgment of what Jesus has done for us. It is being so filled with Jesus that he pours himself out into our thoughts, attitudes, and actions. Our commitment to do the work God has assigned to us is our heartfelt response to that joy.

The knowledge of Jesus that I gained during my long walk with him on the pathway to purpose finally helped me understand what Mother Teresa meant when she described her work in the slums as *pure joy*. There is no doubt that Mother Teresa's source of pleasure and satisfaction was Jesus Christ. He filled her with great gladness that could not be snuffed out, even in the terrible slum conditions in which she lived and labored.

The joy of glorifying God by doing his work can be so powerful that you may wonder if it is wrong—as in sinfully wrong—to feel so extremely satisfied while doing it. This may be particularly true if you feel you don't deserve to be happy, if you were raised to believe that reality is always tough, or if you have thought that ministry is supposed to be a tedious obligation. But believe me, it is not a sin to feel God's pleasure as you fulfill his plans for your life. It is his gift!

In the movie, *Chariots of Fire*, we see a glimpse of the life of Eric Liddell, a devout, early twentieth-century Scottish missionary who also was an Olympic runner. In his efforts to explain his passion for running, Eric said, "When I run I feel his [God's] pleasure." You and I are no different. We may not run, but God has made us—just as he made Eric—to feel his pleasure when we do what he designed us to do.

> *However, I consider my life worth nothing to me, if only I may finish the race and complete the task the Lord Jesus has given me—the task of testifying to the gospel of God's grace.*
> (ACTS 20:24)

This magnificent idea of allowing us to feel joy—to feel fulfilled and satisfied while doing the Lord's work—is to me one of God's most awesome gifts. What a mastermind God is to create us to be most effective and happy when we feel intrinsically useful because we are doing what we love to do. It is the second thing I will thank him for when I get to heaven—the first being his mercy to me through his Son, Jesus Christ.

THERE WILL BE MIRACLES!

Not only will we experience joy as we go about honoring God through the work he has assigned to us, we will find that miracles abound between the last stepping-stone and the bank of the stream. Miracles will help us overcome obstacles, fill us with hope during delays, and guide us to right choices. And we will need every one of them!

Faith heroes of the Bible such as Noah, Abraham, Joseph, and others testify to us that without God's powerful miracles, they would have been doomed! What kinds of miracles did God do to enable his work to be accomplished? Well, in the case of Moses and Joshua, he parted the Red Sea, dropped manna from heaven, sent water gushing forth from rocks in the desert, defeated countless enemies, and more! Likewise, the unparalleled endeavor God has reserved for you will require modern-day miracles and beyond-belief feats that he alone can perform. You may have witnessed miracles before, but those who have lived through this step would say, "Sister, you ain't seen nothin' yet!"

No matter how long it took, or may yet take, to receive your vision from God; no matter how much work you have now that your life purpose is in view, or how ill-prepared you feel, you can trust God—the Creator of all things—to supply your every need. You can expect him to go in front of you to swing open doors that were previously bolted closed. You can expect him to carry you forward on the wings of whatever miracles are needed to complete the task.

Sure, you will still need to do your part, but you are only one character in God's monumental, life-reverberating play. He is the all-knowing playwright, he is the master director, and he will arrange the scene so that you can play your part for his glory. This is not to say that you won't have any problems or trials in this fallen world, but you can count on God to perform unimaginable miracles on your behalf!

As you fulfill your purpose, you'll stand amazed at the majesty of a God who has rescued you from your tiny, limited perspective and placed you strategically in his grand production. It is enough to cause you to raise your hands to the sky in celebration, thrilled that you didn't give up, thrilled that the rock upon which you firmly plant your feet is Almighty God. Being part of something as miraculous as fulfilling the purpose he has assigned to you will cause you to cry out, "Thank you, Jesus, for allowing me, an ordinary woman, to join you where you are at work today. Though I am not worthy, you still chose me and appointed me. Though I am unable, you have equipped me and miraculously paved the way for me to walk. Thank you for the awesome privilege of being used by you."

HANG ON TIGHT!

Do you tend to sneak out the *chicken exit* of roller coaster rides, or do you step forward in line and strap in? At this point on the pathway, I believe God expects there to be no turning back. You have made your commitment to glorify him with your life, and you are meant to keep it. So strap in and hang on tight. You are going on the ride of your life!

It is no longer sufficient to observe Jesus from a distance in the hope of learning something more about godly behavior. It is now a matter of Jesus living inside you and shining through you with all his power, wisdom, and grace. The question is no longer, "What would Jesus do?" but, "How can I cooperate right now with Jesus so that his glory will shine through me?"

This is the time to release your need for control. It is time to step down from your Styrofoam throne and let God take over. His glory will become evident as you choose to listen to his voice and obey his commands. That's why it is so important to learn to obey each of the biblical directives in the growth steps on the pathway to purpose. Every step is critical preparation for magnifying God by following his unique purpose for your life.

> *"You did not choose me, but I chose you and appointed you to go and bear fruit— fruit that will last."* (JOHN 15:16)

It will be all you can do to hang on tight. At times it will feel as if God is moving you forward at supersonic speed and other times at a snail's pace. You may catch yourself screaming with panic as well as delight. Panic may come from the inevitable problems that will test your patience. Delight will come from the sheer exhilaration of taking part in God's glorious plan.

As you well know, I had questions and longings about my purpose that went unanswered for many years. And, you also know that God gave me hints and impressions about his vision for my life that baffled me for years. I had heard, for example, that my pastor, Rick Warren, wanted our church to become one of the most spiritually mature churches in America. I passionately wanted to help in that endeavor, but I didn't know how.

In the meantime, I volunteered at the church and dreamed of being on staff. But I never imagined it would happen. Then, suddenly, I was hired to do sermon research. In true roller coaster fashion, one thing led to another, and I became director of Saddleback's accredited seminary which was one part of the church's spiritual growth plan! My other responsibilities included developing spiritual maturity materials that were intended to help our members become all that God designed them to be. Those tasks, in turn, helped me see the importance of a woman's path toward purpose. What an amazing ride!

When it was the right time in God's plans to perform a majestic miracle regarding the unique dream he had instilled in me to serve the women he adores, he performed it. My primary assignment during the extended process was to hang on, give him the glory, and focus on the tasks he gave me to do each step of the way. Truly, my role was and is to bow before him as my Savior and King and serve him. My responsibility was and is to believe his promise that he does, indeed, have a fascinating plan that involves many exhilarating purposes for my life. My job, as a woman who has known the pain of purposelessness well, is to honor him by sharing the pathway to purpose with other women who seek him.

> *The greatest use of life is to spend it for something that will outlast it.*
> WILLIAM JAMES

THE SOJOURNER'S GUIDE TO BRINGING GLORY TO GOD

The suggestions that follow will help you bring glory to God with every step you take on your pathway to purpose!

Share Your Impressions from God

Erma Bombeck once said, "It takes a lot of courage to show your dreams to someone else." I couldn't agree more. So I urge you to step out in faith and find a "Purpose Partner," a trusted Christian adviser with whom you can share the impressions God has given you about your reasons for being. Don't go through the process alone. Give someone else the privilege of witnessing a miracle-in-the-making with you as you seek to praise the Lord with your life.

Ask God to send you a wise, godly woman who is not only interested in coaching you toward the fulfillment of his vision for your life but is just as interested in your spiritual maturity along the way. As iron sharpens iron, your adviser will sharpen your awareness of what God has called you to do and who he created you to be.

Clean House

Tell the Holy Spirit that you are ready to do some more housekeeping! Let him know that you are cleaning out the lingering cobwebs in the corners of your thought-life and deeds. Ask for his help in taking out the garbage and clutter that are limiting your contribution to God's kingdom.

Choose Joy; Choose Jesus

Do something radical: Choose joy on a minute-by-minute basis in the midst of trials, challenges, setbacks, and even in the midst of your hectic schedule. Decide to be fully devoted to Jesus, the source of highest joy. Believe that he cares about the broken pieces of your life; have regular, meaningful conversations with him; love others; and remind yourself to honor his Father in everything you do. Choose joy by choosing Jesus. Let his love shine through you.

Record the Miracles in a Spiritual Journal

If you don't already have a spiritual journal, you may want to consider getting a notebook or the companion journal to this book

(*Pathway to Purpose for Women Personal Journal*) in which to record God's miracles in your life. Entitle a page in your journal, "Remember the Miracles," and make a list of the significant miracles that God has already performed for you. Leave lots of room on subsequent pages for future entries! The psalmist said, "I will remember the deeds of the Lord; yes, I will remember your miracles of long ago."[4] Get in the habit of recording God's unfathomable ways. Doing this will cause you to recall his strength and majesty when you need him most.

RECOMMENDED BOOKS ON GOD'S MISSION

Designing a Woman's Life, by Judith Couchman[5]

Game Plan, by Bob Buford[6]

Now Is the Time to Bring Glory to God by Completing Your Work

Where are you focusing your life's energy? Is it on something that will bring fame, pleasure, wealth, drama, or power? Or are you applying it to living out God's purposes for you? I urge you to make a commitment to center your life around the daily roles and life purpose goals to which God has called you.

Will you accept his invitation to show up where he is at work every day for the rest of your life? Will you bring with you a passionate desire to glorify, praise, and share him by doing whatever he asks of you? And, just as important, will you serve as a messenger of hope, like the angel Clarence, to all the George Baileys who need a glimpse and more of God's vision for their lives? I pray that your answer to all these questions is yes. I pray that you will take this next step of *bringing glory to God by completing the work he gave you to do.*

Are you beginning to realize that the work God has designed for you today has such a commanding significance that it is worth any sacrifice? I know of no greater privilege than using yourself up to serve God and his eternal purposes. For what, if not that, is worth giving up your life? Nothing. Nothing else even comes close.

When I finally was able to identify what it was God had called me to do, I jotted down what embarking on my unique life purpose felt like:

> The funny thing is, at age forty-seven I feel that God's plans for me are just beginning to accelerate and that the ride with Jesus is going to be a thousand times more joyous, miraculous, fun, and focused than I ever anticipated. Tasting God's purpose for my life has been a treasure chest of hope to me. It is like getting to see God for one split second. I am overwhelmed with gratitude to the point of saying, "I would take one second of experiencing God's will in my life over a hundred years of earthly delight. No doubt about it!"

My prayer for you, taken from Jeremiah 6:16, is that you also will "stand by the roads and look; and ask for the eternal paths, where the good, old way is; then walk in it, and you will find rest for your souls" (AMP). I pray that you won't give up, that you will do whatever it takes to heal and press on, doing today what matters today. I pray that you will be aware of your motives in all that you do. Although I have not walked in your shoes, nor you in mine, I pray that you will realize the need to look out for one another along the pathway. I pray that you will fall hopelessly in love with Jesus, pursue peace, and listen closely to every word he has to say. I pray that you will live a passionate life of full surrender to God, repenting from sin and serving him faithfully for the rest of your life. I pray that you will be filled to overflowing with anticipation, vision, and courage. As you grow into each of God's daily and distinct purposes for your life, I pray that you will blossom into the woman he envisioned you to be before the world began.

I urge you to read this promise from Scripture and pray it for yourself by inserting your name:

I will refresh _____ like the dew from heaven; she will blossom as the lily and root deeply in the soil like cedars in Lebanon. _____'s branches will spread out, as beautiful as olive trees, fragrant as the forests of Lebanon. Her people will return from exile far away and rest beneath my shadow. They will be a watered garden and blossom like grapes and be as fragrant as the wines of Lebanon.[7]

Be confident that God is fulfilling his great purposes through you. May your journey with Jesus be a witness to others of his love and redemption. May you enjoy a phenomenal adventure on the pathway to purpose as the joy of Jesus fills your heart and his purposes fill your days.

GOD'S WISDOM FOR THE PATHWAY

THE "SARAH" STEP OF LIFE: BRINGING GLORY TO GOD BY COMPLETING THE WORK HE GAVE YOU TO DO

For a serious life step lesson from Sarah (who almost missed God's best because of her doubt), read Genesis 18:1–15. Sarah heard (through Abraham and some unnamed visitors) about God's plan for her to have a son. Because she was ninety years old, she laughed and doubted. When God gives you an *impossible* dream, what will your reaction be? Will you bring glory to him by completing the work he gave you to do, regardless of the roadblocks that are God's job to tear down?

Personal Pathway Questions

1. Write any of the steps you have already taken on the pathway to purpose. Checking back through the various chapter exercises, write a three-month goal statement by several steps you have not yet taken or that you need to revisit.

Steps to Take toward Purpose

Forget what is behind and press on toward the goal (Heal and Hope in God's Plan)

Do today what God sent you into the world to do (Current Roles)

Love each other as Jesus loves you (Healthy Relationships)

Seek peace and pursue it (Inner Peace)

Repent and turn away from all your offenses (Changing Your Ways)

Wash one another's feet (Service)

Walk with integrity, not duplicity (Pure Motives)

Expect God to give you the desires of your heart (Passion)

Surrender your everyday, ordinary life before God as an offering (Surrender)

Eagerly anticipate that the Lord God Almighty will reveal his vision to you (Vision)

Take courage (Fear Not)

Bring glory to God by completing the work he gave you to do (Glorify God)

2. What does this verse, Exodus 9:16, say to you? *I have raised you up for this very purpose, that I might show you my power and that my name might be proclaimed in all the earth.*

NOTES

1. (p. 219) See Ephesians 2:10 (from the Greek).

2. (p. 221) Tom Paterson, *Living the Life You Were Meant to Live* (Nashville: Thomas Nelson, 1998), 173.

3. (p. 222) Matthew 25:21.

4. (p. 228) Psalm 77:11.

5. (p. 228) Judith Couchman, *Designing a Woman's Life: A Bible Study and Workbook* (Sisters, Ore.: Multnomah, 1996).

6. (p. 228) Bob Buford, *Game Plan* (Grand Rapids: Zondervan, 1999).

7. (p. 230) Hosea 14:5–7, TLB.

GROUP DISCUSSION GUIDE

HELPFUL TIPS FOR SMALL GROUP USE OR OTHER USES

Though there are thirteen chapters in this book, the discussion guide combines chapters one and two for a twelve-week group study. The number of questions for each "session" (never fewer than seven, never more than eleven) should provide enough study material for about an hour of discussion, depending on the size and talkativeness of your group. Feel free to omit questions or add some of your own. And, of course, build in time to socialize and pray together as best fits your group, setting, and time limitations.

Another idea would be to invite your small group to read the book at its own pace and set a date to get together and discuss each other's insights, much like a book club would do.

You can also use the book with a Purpose Partner (see *Conversations on Purpose for Women*) or at a women's retreat. At a "three main sessions" retreat, the speaker might divide the book as follows: session one, chapters 1–4; session two, chapters 5–8; and session three, chapters 9–13. A "four main sessions" retreat might divide the book: session one, chapters 1–2; session two, chapters 3–6; session three, chapters 7–10; and session four, chapters 11–13.

CHAPTERS 1 AND 2: IS YOUR LIFE OUT OF SYNC? *AND* LEAVE YOUR PAST BEHIND

1. Open your first meeting by inviting group members to talk about one of the questions below that resonates with them:

   ❧ Dear God, where do I fit? How can I make a difference? Where is the place you have for me?

   ❧ Does anyone really need me? Does my existence even matter in this world?

   ❧ Why do I feel like such a failure as a Christian?

   ❧ Why don't I enjoy my church ministry, my family responsibilities, or my job anymore? Why do I feel so unsatisfied?

   ❧ Why am I not happy? How did I pile up so many regrets?

   ❧ Is this really all there is to life? Is this what God wants my life to look like?

   ❧ When did my dreams and passions get relegated to a back burner?

   ❧ If I heard God's call, would I have the time or emotional strength to pursue it?

2. Imagine yourself trying to carry something heavy, perhaps an overloaded backpack or a piggyback rider. What does it feel like to be off-balance from the extra weight? How does carrying "extra emotional weight" from the past affect you today?

3. In what way has your past, both the *good* and the *dealt-with bad*, already had a positive impact on your life? In other words, has it added depth to your character and empathy for God's people? Has it taught you humility or patience? Have you sought forgiveness or learned how to forgive?

4. Describe a time that you have comforted another person with the comfort you yourself have received from God (see 2 Corinthians 1:3–7, especially verse 5). How did that experience alter your understanding of how God works?

5. In what way does your testimony reflect hardship, brokenness, and renewal?

6. Discuss any insights or applications from the story of Mary Magdalene in Luke 8:2 and John 20:1–18 about "forgetting the past and pressing on toward the goal" (see page 40).

7. Which of the following action steps would you like to take this week (pages 37–39)? Why?

   ✍ Write about your pain to help yourself process it

   ✍ Seek professional help

   ✍ Recall a time you healed

   ✍ Prayerfully decide to trust God

   ✍ Write your testimony

   ✍ Ask: To whom will my hurt give hope?

   ✍ Surround yourself with people of hope

CHAPTER 3: DO WHAT MATTERS TODAY

1. Which roles in your life cause you to jump for joy and which cause you to feel plum worn out?

2. Discuss whether you feel that there is a direct correlation between how well you manage your unglamorous, daily efforts and any exciting, larger-than-life purpose later on.

3. Describe a time that God blessed your faithful obedience for doing your *today things*.

4. Recall a time that you applied God's Word to your everyday circumstances. How did that experience affect you? Is that a typical practice for you?

5. Talk about whether you tend to look for greener pastures of more grandiose or dramatic assignments from God, or whether you are content with your present sense of purpose.

6. Discuss any insights or applications about "embracing your current roles" that you glean from the story of Lydia in Acts 16:11–15, 40 (see page 59).

7. What does God want you to be and do in your routine world today?

8. In what ways are you already an official missionary for Christ ("a person sent to do religious or charitable work in some territory") in your home, church, office, school, neighborhood, state, or nation?

9. Which of the following action steps would you like to take this week (pages 57–58)? Why?

    &-Prioritize your roles

    &-Take good care of yourself

    &-Stop the panic

    &-Seize the moment

Chapter 4: Love Others as Jesus Loves You

1. Discuss where you are on this continuum of love. Are you one who already loves others or one who has no desire to learn how to do it? Recall an early example of this in your life.

    0–People, get out of my way or I *will* run over you.

    3–Putting up with certain people sometimes gets me what I want.

    5–Many people are weird, but well worth the investment once I get to know them.

    7–I like most people.

    10–People are precious to me.

2. Has there ever been a time that you attempted to serve without love, share the gospel without love, or grow spiritually without love? Share your experience with the group.

3. How do you feel about this sentence? *Becoming a woman of healthy, loving relationships is a biblical mandate, not just a pleasant suggestion.*

4. Without feeling that you have to give details, talk about how you learned a hard lesson about boundaries, trust, commitment, hatred, bigotry, codependency, abuse, or neglect.

5. Describe your support system in times of discouragement and celebration.

6. Explain whether or not you have *destination disease* (being more concerned about getting to your destination than delighting in the journey with good people).

7. How might perfectionism alienate a woman from loving others?

8. Discuss whether life for you is more like a three-legged race or a game of solitaire.

9. Read the Bible's "love chapter," 1 Corinthians 13. (The *New Living Translation* or *The Message* provides a fresh rendering.) How do the apostle Paul's words echo and build on Jesus' command in John 13:34–35?

10. Which of the following action steps would you like to take this week (pages 71–73)? Why?

    ℰ Catch yourself making a loving difference

    ℰ Get connected at church

    ℰ Offer forgiveness

    ℰ Take a relational opportunities checkup

    ℰ Pray for the unloving and the unlovable

CHAPTER 5: PURSUE PEACE

1. How do you feel about this biblical imperative? *You seek peace, and you pursue it.*

2. Where are you on the Inner Peace Richter Scale?

1	2	3	4	5	6	7	8	9	10
Full-fledged frantic				Semi-serene					At peace

3. Read the story of the two sisters, Mary and Martha, in Luke 10:38–42 (see page 94). Talk about personality type as it affects the idea of "pursuing peace."

4. Discuss this concept: *As a woman of serenity, you will learn how to recognize God's voice, which will make it easier for you to understand your current and long-term assignments from him.*

5. How do you make decisions about family issues, finances, and projects? How would you like to make decisions?

6. What do you believe is the connection among prayer, peace, and purpose?

7. Talk about ways to listen to God as you go about your daily routine. Can you think of a new approach to try this week?

8. In what ways is the pursuit of peace an actual life purpose?

9. Tell about a time that God shared insight with you after you had spent time with him.

10. Which of the following action steps would you like to take this week (pages 91–93)? Why?

    ᪲ Practice silence

    ᪲ Stop the endless mind chatter

    ᪲ Shoot bullet prayers to heaven all day long

    ᪲ Refuse to feel guilty about silence that puts you to sleep or makes you nap

    ᪲ Purposely change your pace

    ᪲ Avoid peace killers

CHAPTER 6: REPENT OF ALL YOUR OFFENSES

1. Review this paragraph from the chapter (page 97):

   The stepping-stone, *repent and turn away from all your offenses*, causes many women to do a hesitation step, almost as if they are taking salsa lessons. (Step forward, left foot. Rock back, right foot.)

   Give a specific example of what your *hesitation step* with repentance has looked like in the past.

2. What do you believe is the connection between your character formation (less sinning, more repenting, and more obedience) and a distinct life purpose?

3. What lifestyle change has repentance caused for you at some point in your life?

4. What proactive steps do you recommend to avoid or resist temptation?

5. In what way do you identify with the universal sins mentioned by the young inmates?

   - Selfishness
   - Jealousy
   - Self-doubt
   - Stubbornness
   - Greed
   - Laziness
   - Judgmental attitude
   - Rage
   - Addictions/obsessions
   - Instant gratification

6. Read about Jesus' conversation with the Samaritan woman in John 4:4–42. (Verses 7–29 provide the core of the story.) What initial evidence of the woman's repentance is evident in this passage of Scripture?

7. What is the most dramatic change you have witnessed in someone's life as a result of his or her repentance?

8. Which of the following action steps would you like to take this week (pages 107–110)? Why?

    🍂 Turn toward God

    🍂 Memorize a Scripture

    🍂 Consider the consequences of your sin

    🍂 Consider missed blessings

    🍂 Accept reproof

    🍂 Be honest with yourself about specific sins

    🍂 Pray a prayer

CHAPTER 7: WASH ONE ANOTHER'S FEET

1. Has anyone in your group actually washed someone's feet or clipped toenails other than their own children's? Describe the experience. If not, describe a similar experience of hands-on service that was personally demanding.

2. Read the account of Jesus washing his disciples' feet in John 13:1–17. What insights about service do you glean from this passage, especially verses 13–17?

3. How do you feel about this concept introduced by Henry Blackaby and Claude King? *Watch to see where God is at work and join him.* What challenges and/or opportunities could this create for you?

4. When and how did you learn that being of humble service to others was one of God's purposes for your life?

5. Think of an example in which God worked mightily to enlarge the influence and ministry of someone who obeyed him.

6. Describe your experience with learning empathy and patience, as you have taken steps toward fulfilling your purposes.

7. Where are you in the process of discovering your spiritual giftedness?

8. Talk about one thing you have learned from a church ministry or mission opportunity.

9. Share an example of an *obedience homerun* (immediately doing what God requests with a positive attitude) from your own life or the life of another.

10. Which of the following action steps would you like to take this week (pages 126–128)? Why?

&Seize an opportunity to give yourself away

&Think long term about serving

&Stay balanced; retain some margin

&Take a spiritual gifts inventory

&Try on new ministry shoes

CHAPTER 8: WALK WITH INTEGRITY

1. What are some of your motives for wanting God to reveal your unique life purpose (for example: to satisfy curiosity, to give you bragging rights, or to serve God and others)? Did you discover any hidden motives as you reflected on this chapter?

2. How could gossip be a destructive underlying reason for a prayer request?

3. Without naming names or identifiable circumstances, have you ever witnessed a lack of integrity in someone that led to cheating, envy, slander, scheming, malice, flattery, treachery, or secret wickedness? What were the worst repercussions of the person's duplicity?

4. Consider the following impure motives that could cause serious damage to a relationship: the desire to manipulate a situation, control an opinion, seek revenge, stir up trouble, embarrass someone, or show off talent, beauty, or knowledge. When we recognize these motives in ourselves, how could we cooperate with God to counteract them?

5. Read these three Scripture verses about motives: 1 Chronicles 28:9; Proverbs 16:2; and 1 Corinthians 4:5. Discuss the primary concepts presented there.

6. Recall a time when you or someone you know has been driven by a motive of guilt. Knowing what you know today, how would you handle that situation differently or advise someone else to do so?

7. Which of the following action steps would you like to take this week (pages 142–143)? Why?
   - Ask God for a specific example about your motives
   - Ask a friend for specifics about your motives
   - Offer your impure motives to God

CHAPTER 9: EXPECT THE DESIRES OF YOUR HEART

1. What is your understanding of the meaning of Psalm 37:4? *Delight yourself in the* LORD *and he will give you the desires of your heart.* Read the context of David's words in Psalm 37:1–6.

2. In what way do you struggle with any of these feelings?
   - I don't deserve to receive the extravagant reward of living passionately.
   - Passions are one of Satan's traps to coax me into wanting secular rewards.
   - God probably won't give me what I really want.

3. What is your overarching view of God: Intimidating ruler of the universe? Righteous judge? Powerful king? Abba/Pappa? Other? How does your view of God help or hinder your ability to live with healthy passions?

4. What response would you give to someone who asked you these questions:
   - Why would God allow me, a serious sinner, to do what I love doing?
   - What if God doesn't approve of my deepest, healthy desires?

5. How do healthy passions help protect you against addictions?

6. What do you believe is the connection between a woman's healthy passions and God's purposes in her life? Discuss one of your passions and any connections you see to God's purposes for you.

7. Which of the following action steps would you like to take this week (pages 158–160)? Why?

   &- Use some basic hints from chapter nine to get started

   &- Guard against jealousy of others

   &- Daydream

   &- Go for it—experiment

CHAPTER 10: SURRENDER YOUR DAILY LIFE TO GOD

1. Does surrendering to God frighten or excite you? In what way?

2. How do you feel about this general concept? *God owns all creation, including you and me. Our lives are simply on loan to us. We are stewards of what he has entrusted to us.*

3. Describe some modern-day idols that seem alluring to you. (Idols include anything that takes a higher priority than God in your life—anything you hold tightly in your fist.) What are some ways to overcome such idolatry?

4. Read the story of the angel Gabriel's visit with Mary in Luke 1:26–38 (see page 179). Discuss any insights and applications about surrender that you gain from this Scripture passage.

5. Why do you think it is important to surrender what you dream of doing for God?

6. How does the spiritual practice of surrender prepare you for your future assignments from God?

7. In what way is *waving a white flag of surrender to God* a victory?

8. When and how did you first realize that surrender was a distinct, tangible, assigned purpose for today? What impact does that realization have on you?

9. Talk about a time when you or someone you know surrendered something to God and then had the Magnificent Counselor guide his or her next steps.

10. Would you still love God and follow him if he actually took everything that you surrendered to him?

11. Which of the following action steps would you like to take this week (pages 175–177)? Why?
    - Seek the truth
    - Do your footwork and homework
    - Count the cost
    - Think with the mind of Christ
    - Publicly give up control of your will
    - Prayerfully begin
    - Take a "one-day surrender challenge"

CHAPTER 11: ANTICIPATE GOD'S VISION

1. Discuss whether you *eagerly anticipate that the Lord God Almighty will reveal his vision to you.*

2. What if God sent you a message on a tape recorder or called to you in an audible voice: "This is your mission for the rest of your life. You will honor me, should you choose to accept it"? Would you accept it? Are you already accepting it? Explain.

3. Recall a time you might have asked any of these three questions:
    - What if I am doing something wrong that is preventing God from speaking to me?
    - What if God already revealed his vision to me, and I missed it?
    - What if I heard God's thoughts, but I don't want to do what he told me to do?

4. In what ways do you feel God is giving you a glimpse of his vision for your life, of the humanly impossible task he has in mind for you?

5. Which of the Bible men or women of vision mentioned in the box on page 192 particularly inspires you? Why?

6. How would you feel about a visionary task from God that made you look foolish in the eyes of the world (like Noah, who built an ark on dry land)?

7. To what extent have you prepared for and begun to fulfill God's vision for your life? Have you asked God to reveal his vision; admitted that you have seen it; sought advice amidst your confusion; or begun the work after you got your instructions?

8. How do you feel about receiving a vision that will cost you your life in the sense that you must choose to die to self and accept God's plan—and in the sense that you will be spent and all used up by him?

9. Share about whether you really believe that God will cause an epiphany in your life, that he will demonstrate plainly who he is and how you can worship him with your life.

10. Which of the following action steps would you like to take this week (pages 196–197)? Why?

    🖎 Pray and ask others to pray that God will reveal his vision for your life

    🖎 Be confident

    🖎 Practice patience

    🖎 Ask God to speak to you

CHAPTER 12: TAKE COURAGE

1. If you feel comfortable doing so, share about one of your fears.

2. Tell about a time that God used you in spite of your fear.

3. What do you most dislike about your fear? (For example, does it block creativity, productivity, or relationships in your life?)

4. Share about a time when you persevered through fear. How did God use that experience in your life?

5. Discuss which of these fears is most prevalent today in your life or in the life of others: fear of ridicule and criticism, fear of success, fear of being found out, fear of failure.

6. Read Isaiah 43:1–5. What does this summarized version of that passage say to you? *Fear not, for I have redeemed you; I have summoned you by name; you are mine. Do not be afraid, for I am with you.*

7. Share about a courageous person you have read about or known.

8. In what circumstance is God currently asking you to *walk on water* toward him, keeping your eyes focused on him?

9. Which of the following action steps would you like to take this week (pages 213–215)? Why?

    ❧ Use the fear hierarchy approach and give your fears to God one by one

    ❧ Ask yourself about the self-focus that fear causes and about what fear steals from you

    ❧ Use the "just eat your spinach" approach

    ❧ Feed your courage with the Word of God

CHAPTER 13: BRING GLORY TO GOD

1. Do you feel you are getting a late start toward fulfilling your mission for God? Explain.

2. Read the story of Sarah's "impossible dream" in Genesis 18:10–15 and its fulfillment in Genesis 21:1–7 (see page 230). Discuss any insights or applications you can take away from these Scripture passages.

3. From your perspective, what miracles will be required for you to complete the work God has given you to do?

4. What would be the most challenging aspect of inscribing your life symphony with *SDG* (the Latin *Soli Deo Gloria*, meaning "to God alone be the glory")?

5. When have you fallen to your knees and cried out, "Thank you, Jesus, for allowing me, an ordinary woman, the privilege of being used by you"?

6. Share about how difficult it has been to balance and manage your time, energy, resources, spiritual growth, talents, character, experiences, and roles. Do you look forward to all of it converging into God's plan for your life?

7. Talk about whether you have experienced the pure joy of Jesus as you live out your life mission.

8. Which of the following action steps would you like to take this week (pages 227–228)? Why?

    - Share your impressions from God
    - Clean house again
    - Choose joy; choose Jesus
    - Record the miracles in a spiritual journal

9. Review all the action steps in the previous chapters. Share one that you took and how it made a difference for you. (For your easy reference, use this Group Discussion Guide's chapter summary questions.)

Fresh Start with Jesus

Therefore God exalted him [Jesus] to the highest place and gave him
the name that is above every name, that at the name of Jesus every knee
should bow, in heaven and on earth and under the earth, and every tongue
confess that Jesus Christ is Lord, to the glory of God the Father.
(PHILIPPIANS 2:9–11)

Over the course of reading this book, have you agreed to let Jesus be your Savior? If you are ready to take the first step today on the pathway to purpose, here's a simple prayer you can say:

Jesus, I believe that you died for me and that God raised you from
the dead. Please forgive my sins. You are my Savior. You are my only
hope. I want to follow your will for my life. I bow and confess that
you, Jesus Christ, are Lord.

If you decided just now to accept Jesus as your Savior and Lord, you are assured forever of salvation. Nothing can snatch you now from the hand of God. Please let someone know about your decision, so he or she can encourage you and thank God for his grace-filled, purposeful plan for your life.

If you decided not to say the prayer, I urge you to mark this page and to keep seeking truth with an open heart and mind. If you need

help, ask a pastor or a Christian friend. Some Scripture verses that I
highly recommend are these:

Romans 3:23	All have sinned.
Romans 6:23	Heaven is a free gift.
Romans 5:8	Jesus has already, out of love for you, paid the penalty for your sins by dying on the cross.
Romans 10:9–10	If you confess that Jesus is Lord, and if you tell God that you believe he raised Jesus from the dead, you will be saved.
Romans 10:13	Ask God to save you by his grace. He will!

Acknowledgments

To all those who walked alongside me during some or all of the fifteen years it took to write this book:

My countless prayer warriors, especially Gwen Kennedy, who was relentless. Linda Smith, who verified every Scripture reference, long into the evenings. Anita Renfroe, my talented humor consultant. My most serious and helpful critics: Jessie Mikolaski, Maura Ewing, Ina Miller, Jim and Lena Campbell, Maria McNeill, Janet Pound, Denise Paley, and Susan Waterman. Some of my LifePlan clients (dear friends) who were dedicated to breathing insight into the manuscript: Lisa Kuecker, Clara Yang, Colleen Bowen, and Carol Travilla. And especially the incomparable quartet of Lynne Ellis, Linda Kaye, Suzanne Montgomery, and Tobin Perry, who each tackled some of the toughest revisions over the years. And most gratefully, Pastor Doug Fields, who poured his insight and love into this project at an *impossible* time in his life.

My niece, Alicia Nishioka, who in 1993 was the first "cover" artist to tackle the pre-contracted assignment. Sharon Wood, who then designed my first seminar workbook. Katie Keller, who said in 1994, "I believe God wants you to do this. Please don't quit." Cathy Workman, who began storing manuscript disks for me in 1995 when she was in junior high school. Philip Hamer and Benson Bird, who as high school kids in 1997 edited my first video presentation for a publisher. And Matt McGill, a Saddleback pastor, who in 2000 urged me to follow the vision God gave me.

My beloved traveling companion—my mom—as well as my dear dad and seven brothers and sisters, who each ministered to me in his or her own way. My brother Mark for reading and commenting on "his sister's book for women." My sister Terri for the *Believe* sweatshirt she gave me years ago that speaks of her lifelong message to me. My sister Cathy for letting me practice my first LifePlan facilitation on her! And beyond all measure, my sister Maureen, for her incredible gift of narrative writing and kindnesses as she devoted countless hours to endless drafts.

Nancy Jernigan, my miracle-worker agent—who believes unwaveringly in God's joy-filled plan for my life. And, I know that God's favor was on me when he selected my Zondervan team: Darwin Rader and Greg Stielstra, my wise and visionary marketing managers; Greg Clouse, my patient, focused developmental editor; Cindy Davis and Beth Shagene, my cover and interior designers; Jeff Bowden, my audio book producer; Jaime Seaton, my phenomenal national account sales manager—all standing on the capable shoulders of the entire Zondervan in-house and field staff. It definitely took a small village of professionals to release five products simultaneously. And, most humbly, Cindy Hays Lambert, senior executive acquisitions editor, my godly sojourner, whose wisdom and strategic thinking are incomparable.

And, incalculably, Amanda Sorensen, my freelance editor, for her relentless pursuit of excellence in wordsmithing and concept alignment. She was God's answer to my seven-year prayer for a woman's voice that could enhance my efforts for clarity and pacing!

Thank you all so much for your love in action. I treasure your friendship and gratefully acknowledge your enormous contribution to this book.

How to Contact the Author

To reach Katie Brazelton, Ph.D.,
founder of *Pathway to Purpose™ Ministry*,
regarding a speaking engagement,
upcoming seminar,
church consultation,
LifePlan referral or facilitator training,
or to read about her upcoming books
or her dream of opening Women's
Life Purpose Coaching™ Centers,
please visit her website at

www.pathwaytopurpose.com.

Or write to:

Saddleback Church
Katie Brazelton
1 Saddleback Parkway
Lake Forest, CA 92630

To inquire about **any of the women contributors**
in this book series
or to learn more about any of the topics addressed,
please visit the author's website.

The Purpose-Driven® Life
What On Earth Am I Here For?

Over 20 million copies sold
New York Times Bestseller

RICK WARREN

THE PURPOSE DRIVEN Life

WHAT ON EARTH AM I HERE FOR?

A GROUNDBREAKING MANIFESTO ON THE MEANING OF LIFE!

The most basic question everyone faces in life is *Why am I here? What is my purpose?* Self-help books suggest looking within, at your own desires and dreams, but Rick Warren says that is the wrong place to start. You must begin with God—and his eternal purposes for your life. Real meaning and significance don't come from pursuing human goals but from understanding and fulfilling God's purposes for putting you on earth. This book will help you understand God's incredible plan for your life. You'll see "the big picture" of what life is all about and begin to live the life God created you to live.

The Purpose-Driven® Life is a manifesto for Christian living in the 21st century—a lifestyle based on eternal purposes, not cultural values. Using biblical stories and letting the Bible speak for itself, Warren clearly explains God's five purposes for each of us:

- You were planned for God's pleasure—so your first purpose is to experience *real worship.*
- You were formed for God's family—so your second purpose is to enjoy *real fellowship.*
- You were created to become like Christ—so your third purpose is to learn *real discipleship.*
- You were shaped for serving God—so your fourth purpose is to practice *real ministry.*
- You were made for a mission—so your fifth purpose is to live out *real evangelism.*

Written in a captivating devotional style, the book is divided into 40 short chapters that can be read as a daily devotional, studied by small groups, and used by churches participating in the nationwide *"40 Days of Purpose"* campaign.

Rick Warren is the founding pastor of Saddleback Church in Lake Forest, California, a congregation that averages 20,000 in attendance each weekend. He is the author of four books, and founder of Pastors.com, a global Internet community for those in ministry.

ISBN: 0-310-20571-9

All Pathway to Purpose™ books work together to enhance a woman's journey as she searches for her God-given purpose. Each book provides its own unique benefit that enriches her walk down the pathway.

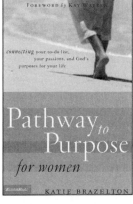

Pathway to Purpose™ for Women is a standalone book that takes the five universal purposes from *The Purpose-Driven® Life* and helps women drill down to their own unique life purposes. This book is also available as an Abridged Audio CD.

Conversations on Purpose for Women is a companion book to *Pathway to Purpose for Women*, specifically designed for those women who want to find another woman who can serve as their Purpose Partner to help them down the path toward purpose.

Praying for Purpose for Women is a 60-day prayer experience that can change a woman's life forever. Sixty influential Christian women share how *their* lives have changed.

Pathway to Purpose™ for Women Personal Journal allows women to reflect during their quiet time on how the principles they discover can and will affect their lives.

Pathway to Purpose™ for Women	ISBN: 0-310-25649-6
(In Spanish) *Camino hacia el propósito para mujeres*	ISBN: 08297-4506-8
Pathway to Purpose™ for Women Abridged Audio CD	ISBN: 0-310-26505-3
Conversations on Purpose for Women	ISBN: 0-310-25650-X
(In Spanish) *Conversaciones con propósito para mujeres*	ISBN: 08297-4508-4
Praying for Purpose for Women	ISBN: 0-310-25652-6
(In Spanish) *Oración con propósito para mujeres*	ISBN: 08297-4507-6
Pathway to Purpose™ for Women Personal Journal	ISBN: 0-310-81174-0

Spanish products available May, 2005.

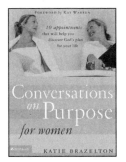
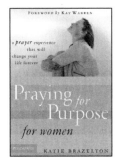

We want to hear from you. Please send your comments about this book to us in care of zreview@zondervan.com. Thank you.

ZONDERVAN™

GRAND RAPIDS, MICHIGAN 49530 USA

WWW.ZONDERVAN.COM